INTERVENTION

●

The Battle for Better Business

Elliot H. Forte

ISBN 978-1-4478-6323-6

Jacket by www.advisio.co.uk

Cover image © Advisio Limited

ACKNOWLEDGMENTS

To all those people who have challenged my thinking, I am sincerely grateful. I have been privileged to work with leaders of over 3,000 small businesses in England and consider each and every one worthy of my utmost respect. I will always be thankful for the time and their enthusiasm to embrace new ideas. I have learnt something new from every one of these people and humbly thank them all.

Intervention in small business is a complex and controversial topic, which inevitably stimulates difference of opinion. I am particularly grateful to Rt Hon the Lord Heseltine CH who agreed to contribute to this story of business support. This book would not have happened without this stimulus and his forthright opinions on government intervention. This meeting was akin to the Chairman of Tesco granting a one to one audience with a till cashier.

On a personal note I am grateful to trusted colleagues who gave up their time to support and challenge this project, particularly Jonathan Sharp. I would like to recognise Yvette Coles and Tony Rusbridge for their contribution and to thank all the people I had the privilege of working alongside at Business Link over the past twenty years, who without exception cared passionately about helping small businesses prosper. If I have not acknowledged them in the text, it only means they have entered my thoughts in subliminal fashion.

Thanks also to Trevor Lansdown of Word Engineers for his valuable advice.

Most of all I would like to thank my wife Samantha Forte who always supports my ideas (however outlandish) yet never fails to speak her mind. I would not be here without Sam and our children.

CONTENTS

INTRODUCTION

Intervention is the story of Government funded business support and the impact these policies had on small and medium sized businesses for a generation.

The degree of Government intervention in the affairs of business is rooted deeply in political persuasion. It is fundamentally a clash of ideas between those on the right who believe in a laissez faire economy (survival of the fittest) and those on the left who veer towards a more planned industrial policy. This pendulum swings back and forwards depending on which political party holds power.

In 1992, Lord Heseltine, then President of the Board of Trade, led an unprecedented change to industrial policy in the United Kingdom. John Major's Conservative Government had been returned to power and the post Thatcher recession of the early nineties was at a peak. It was in this challenging economic landscape that the Competitiveness White Paper was conceived. This blatantly interventionist strategy acknowledged the uncomfortable truth that Britain was no longer an economic superpower and was continuing to fall behind our European peers. More significantly, the paper concluded that rather than large faceless corporations, it would be the small and medium sized business sector that would be the saviour of the economy.

The Government was no longer prepared to remain a passive observer whilst the economic fortunes of Britain declined. A series of measures were announced to stimulate enterprise, the most significant investment being the set up of a national network of Business Link organisations.

Business Link would offer impartial and independent advice to small and medium sized businesses and would address an assumed market failure. The Government believed organisations were not receiving adequate help from private sector business support and in the absence of affordable quality advice, would step in to be a "business friend." The taxpayer would fund people on the ground able to offer face-to-face advice on growing a business. These business advisers would be backed up by a library of information and where appropriate, grant funding. The launch of Business Link received rare cross party political support and was welcomed by existing private sector bodies such as the Chamber of Commerce, Federation of Small Businesses and Confederation of British Industry. However, despite this early support the Business Link model ultimately received sustained and voracious criticism from these stakeholders. In 2008, Dragon's Den entrepreneur Doug Richard finally wrote the death note for Business Link in his Conservative Party funded paper "The Richard Report." These critiques are reviewed and examined in detail to prepare a more balanced picture of intervention in private business.

This book tells the story of Government funded support through the eyes of the largest business support organisation in history, Business Link. At its peak Business Link was helping over 750,000 small and medium sized businesses each year and achieving customer satisfaction exceeding 90%. However, statistics only tell one story. This book exposes the real impact changing Government support policy had on small business entrepreneurs, in both a boom and bust Britain. The key stakeholders in this story are named and their actual contributions to small business performance are ruthlessly examined. After analysing the past twenty years of Business Link activity, key learning is captured and published for small businesses and partners alike. Valuable and expensive lessons which would otherwise have been scattered to the wind when the Business Link advisory service closed on November 25th, 2011.

I passionately believe it is in the interest of everyone involved in enterprise to understand how the forces of Government intervention evolved, how they were managed and ultimately how the Country returned to a survival of the fittest mentality. Intervention offers small businesses great opportunities to improve their performance. However, private and public funded business support is a lucrative sector and it is right to question whether decisions were always in the interests of the small business entrepreneur. Knowing the difference can be advantageous and profitable. This book also highlights the perpetual ebb and flow of intervention, which causes a permanent state of uncertainty and reinvention depending on the political influence of the day.

I hold a view that business support, be it private or public funded, has made a significant difference to millions of businesses in the United Kingdom. However, after seventeen years at the coalface, I am resolute in my belief that small businesses deserve much better and have an undeniable right to ask why taxpayer funding is invested in their name.

Intervention - the Battle for Better Business, is my humble attempt to empower the entrepreneurs of small and medium sized businesses, to ask them to demand more in a time where less is the new norm. I hope this book helps demystify the maze of business support, particularly for small business entrepreneurs, the foundation of our economy and the acorns that become oaks.

Elliot Forte

Personal Business Adviser

Business Link - 1996 to 2011

....

www.battleforbetterbusiness.co.uk

CHAPTER ONE

SHOOTS AND ROOTS

1992

"You create the world class companies. But in a thousand ways, the decisions that we take in Government can help you or hinder you. So we too are part of Britain's competitiveness. All our policies – not just our economic policy – need to be focused on the future strength of the British economy."

John Major
The Prime Minister
Confederation of British Industry (CBI) Annual Dinner 1993

100 Years of Decline

Despite everyone's best efforts for the best part of half a century, the United Kingdom had fallen from third in real income per head in 1950 to tenth in Europe by the 1980's. Shortly after the Second World War productivity in manufacturing had been 10% higher than Germany and double the performance of Japan. In 1979, Japanese productivity had exceeded our own by 33%. Worse still the Germans had achieved a 50% higher performance. In just 30 years the UK's share of world export halved.

Despite a period of rapid growth during the 1980's, fuelled in part by a Government programme of privatisation and tax cuts, a grim reality was becoming part of the public consciousness, particularly in government circles. The UK still lagged significantly behind their international rivals. It was this steady economic decline that faced the re-elected Conservative Party in 1992, when a slim majority returned John Major to power.

The Rise of the Small Firm

In the 1980's a significant change occurred in the structure of the UK economy. The brutal optimism of Thatcher economic policy had fuelled a spike in "try and do" behaviour, and a risk-embracing boom.

In 1979, businesses employing less than 100 people made up 40% of non-government employment. By 1994, this figure had increased to 50% and over 10 million people were part of the small firms explosion. Despite the recession of the early 1990's, this bumper crop of acorn businesses was now key to the future growth of the British economy.

It was in this context that the Competitiveness Agenda was born.

Telling you what you think

Government economic policy is constantly seeking new ways to address changes in the trading landscape, reacting to the views and needs of businesses, the corporate electorate. These views are significantly influenced by a combination of independent research and lobbying. Primarily, the Government's ear is open to business groups including the Confederation of British Industry (CBI), the Chamber of Commerce and Federation of Small Businesses. These organisations claim to represent the views of British entrepreneurs and speak for all small businesses, whether they are members or not.

In 1992, John Major's Government was listening hard, forming their own ideal of the small business owner and their needs.

Small Business Mind

The new Competitiveness Agenda was the brainchild of Lord Heseltine who in 1992 was appointed President of the Board of Trade (Department of Trade and Industry).

The Government concluded that small businesses have "exceptional drive and determination to succeed." They believed small businesses were flexible to customer demands, had the ability to respond quickly, offered flexibility and choice and they were not afraid to take on the jobs too small for larger companies. However, the Government concluded all was not rosy for British small business. In their view 'every day' demands of doing the work and winning new business blinded small businesses to the future. They didn't really plan ahead or think to invest in training for tomorrow. They relied on a small number of customers and always seemed to be facing some sort of cash crisis. The Government considered small businesses to be cautious, their instinct being that borrowing money was just too much of a risk. Finally, they concluded paperwork was a monkey on the back of all businesses, and that smaller organisations fervently despised regulations and tax. Sound familiar? Remarkably this debate has been ongoing for the best part of half a century. A bank of expensive research is tribute to stating the obvious.

Welcome to Competitiveness

Many people in the business community were then and are still precious about the title of entrepreneur. As if to prove the point a vast plethora of studies and reports have been created over the past thirty years (funded from both public and private sector pots) trying to encapsulate what it means to earn the title of "entrepreneur." Chuck in a large shot of new millennium media and the title seems to be the sole domain of fire-breathing dragons.

In the context of Competitiveness, if you were a person who had shown enough initiative to start up in business, you were an entrepreneur. If you had to wake up every morning and think how to create something (or survive), you were taking risks, however seemingly insignificant. There were *no* decisions in business without risk and you deserved respect. *You* were an entrepreneur. Of course you may be a very poor entrepreneur, but that doesn't make you any less deserving of the title, whatever people might have you believe.

Prevention and Intervention

"For a firm, competitiveness is the ability to produce the right goods and services of the right quality, at the right price, at the right time. It means meeting customers' needs more efficiently and more effectively than other firms."

Competitiveness: Helping Business to Win
Published 31ˢᵗ December, 1994, by Department of Trade and Industry

During 1993 and 1994, the Government was in the process of completing their very first Competitiveness White Paper. White papers declare in advance what will be done in the name of government, or in this case the Department of Trade and Industry. For good reason these documents are called Command papers.

On 31ˢᵗ December, 1994, the Department of Trade and Industry published "Competitiveness: Helping Business to Win." This seminal document would dictate government economic policy for small businesses for a generation.

Industrial strategy shifted focus squarely onto smaller business with a recognition that 96% of businesses actually employed less than 20 people. This represented 33% of private sector employment. Compared to our International rivals, this segment of the business community was growing at an exponential rate. Equally important to the new strategy was a belief that innovation was going to be key in future markets, and that small businesses would be a vital cog in the wheel. As a result, the Government proclaimed that the route back to competitiveness would be through nurturing and growing the seedbed of acorn enterprises in the UK.

Positive Action

The Government believed it was insufficient to rely solely on market forces to help small businesses prosper and flourish. Rather, they held the view that a series of market failures required clear and present intervention.

The Competitiveness command paper promised small and medium sized businesses:

- Tax relief
- Deregulation
- Support with finance
- Information and advice
- Support for consultancy
- Delivering management best practice
- Skills and training

The signs of intervention creep had been there for all to see over the previous decade. Prior to 1993, a number of "successful" interventions had already been targeted at the small business sector.

INTRODUCTION BY THE PRIME MINISTER

I have many ambitions for our country. I want to see higher living standards for our families, better schools and hospitals, strong defence, a cleaner environment, and a thriving artistic and cultural national life. All these depend on the success of the private wealth creating sector. To obtain a better quality of life for all, and to keep taxes as low as possible, we need our businesses to succeed.

Today, our companies face the most competitive environment they have ever seen. Change is relentless and swift. The global financial market never sleeps. Technology has shrunk the world. Free trade has opened new markets but it has also created new competitors. We cannot ignore these changes. To do so means certain decline.

We seek success from good foundations. We now have better industrial relations than ever before and our productivity is at an all time high. Inflation and interest rates are at historically low levels. But to make the most of these advantages we must continually improve our standards.

I am determined to set the framework for long-term success. We must prepare this country for the changing and challenging world of the next century. My aim is to create a climate in which our companies can beat the best. That is what this White Paper is all about.

Our first duty is to continue to win the battle against inflation. Low inflation has brought lower interest rates. It creates its own dynamic for investment and growth.

Second, I believe we must give our young people the highest standards of education and training. Their skills will be the key to our future. Education and training have undergone great but necessary change. This White Paper contains important new proposals to expand opportunity and to raise standards still higher.

Our aim is commercial and industrial success and the rewards it will bring for all of us. To achieve this we seek a new partnership between Government and industry – a partnership for prosperity in a competitive world.

John Major

Introduction sourced from Competitiveness: Helping Business to Win
Published 31st December, 1994, by Department of Trade and Industry

Intervention to Support Consultancy

The Enterprise Initiative (1988 to 1994) evolved from a perceived market failure in the business support sector. These concerns were founded on statistics that demonstrated a poor take up of external advice by small businesses, or to put it more simply, not enough people were paying consultants to buy-in added expertise. The market failure was explained as small businesses underestimating the benefits of using external advice, implying the entrepreneur was at fault. In reality, the consultancy sector had historically served a minority of organisations (the successful ones with cash) and, if there was any failure, it was the sales ability of consultants themselves. Therefore, the Enterprise Initiative was designed to "encourage" take up of external advice by making it a more attractive proposition. A significant element of the Enterprise Initiative would be free money.

Any British business with less than 500 personnel could apply for this package of support and, surprisingly enough, 'free money' is a product that sells pretty well. In a single year (1993) a total of 17,995 grant applications were received. Over ten thousand were processed successfully. When the scheme closed in 1994, the initiative had received 135,700 applications for grants, with over 65,000 awards.[1] Some years after the initiative an independent Wren and Storey report assessed the Marketing element of the scheme. The report concluded that each £1,000 of grant assistance increased sales £30,000 and created one new job.[2] An alternative study by Bennett and Robson estimated that this initiative trebled the take up of external advice in the small business population (engagement had been 10% originally). [3] The main lesson learnt by government was that grant provision increases the number of businesses buying external advice. A more significant and far-reaching lesson learnt in the business community was, if I don't want to risk my own money, the taxpayer is willing do it for me. Understandably, this was a view unlikely to be discouraged by many people trying to make a living in the consultancy sector.

If you were a business and didn't want to pay a consultant (or were unable), the taxpayer would now pick up the bill. Ta very much. Well almost. As part of the deal a small business had to use one of the Government's "approved" consultants (the first of an ever reincarnating database of suppliers) and be rubber stamped by one of the schemes advisers - a small price to pay to get some hard earned tax back.

A grants culture was born which prevails to this day, particularly in smaller businesses facing cash challenges on a day-to-day basis.

Tomorrow's Company

The Competitiveness Agenda went on to define exactly what was to be expected of small business entrepreneurs in the future. In "Tomorrow's Company", the White Paper of 1994 demanded:

- Be clear about your purpose and values
- Meet and exceed customer demands
- Learn fast and change fast
- Inspire people to new levels of skill, efficiency and creativity
- Create a shared destiny with all stakeholders (customers, employees etc.)
- Recognise concentration on one stakeholder will not lead to competitiveness
- Use relevant performance measures

A key competence needed in tomorrow's company was isolated - management. The Government believed management skills in small businesses were variable and certainly not comprehensive. No one exactly fell off his or her chair to hear this revelation. However, at least some of the mind fog had been blown away. Small businesses now had a single source of competitive advantage to target and could apply some concentrated, focused effort.

The White Paper reaffirmed that small business managers were fiercely independent and wary of seeking external support. Even when a small business manager did feel the need for support, it was deemed that they would not know where to start, the business support sector being a "patchwork quilt" of providers with no market leader.

The Department of Trade and Industry would not stand idly by in the face of this market failure, being so critical to the future of Britain PLC. As a result the White Paper committed to:

- Help small businesses recognise the "need for change"
- Encourage sharing of information
- Communicate best management practice
- Provide "effective access to a wide range of business services."

With these pledges the shoots of an interventionist policy were firmly rooted. Intervention was no longer a choice; it was a necessity in the national interest.

One-Stop-Shop

Lord Heseltine's concept of a one-stop shop was not a new one. Indeed, each of the main political parties had made a commitment to the concept in their 1992 election manifestos.

"Small and growing businesses will have a new deal. They need the backing on which their competitors can rely in France and Germany. Labour will establish a network of one-stop advice centres providing them with access to high quality specialist assistance."

Source: It's Time to Get Britain Working Again, 1992 Labour Party Manifesto

"We will encourage small business and the self-employed, and ensure a level playing field with their larger counterparts ... and encourage Training and Enterprise Councils, chambers of commerce and local enterprise agencies to reorganise to form a network of business-led one-stop-shops."

Source: Changing Britain for Good, 1992 Liberal Democrat Party Manifesto

"Small businesses are the seed corn of the economy ... during the new Parliament we will develop a new Enterprise Service to give small and medium sized businesses help in diagnosing their most important strategic needs. A new Consultancy Brokerage Service will supply information to small companies."

Source: The Best Future for Britain, 1992 Conservative Party Manifesto

It was with no little sarcasm that Lord Heseltine, than President of the Board of Trade, acknowledged cross party support for a one-stop-shop in the House of Commons.

"I do not know how it got in the Labour Party manifesto, but it did. Before the right hon. Gentleman gets carried away, I shall point out that it was also featured in the Liberal manifesto. If there is one thing that creates anxiety in my mind, it is that I introduced an idea to which both main Opposition parties subscribe!"

Michael Heseltine MP, President of the Board of Trade
House of Commons Hansard Debate 5th April, 1995

Driving the Stakeholders

Training and Enterprise Councils (TECs) had been launched in 1990, replacing the Manpower Services Commission. Each TEC was tasked to make a key contribution to the performance of their local economy; both through their own activities to improve business competitiveness and develop workforce skills, and by taking a lead in co-coordinating local action. Over a thousand local business and community leaders were members of TEC Boards. By 1992, TECs had developed a wide range of services serving over 150,000 small businesses per annum. There were 82 TECs in England and Wales, managing a budget of £1.8 billion of public funding.

The gauntlet of simplifying the business support sector was thrown at the feet of these employer-led organisations, the mythical "one stop shop" for small and medium sized businesses. This was an unenviable task due to the number of differing stakeholder groups active in the business support sector.

All the business support organisations acknowledged the need for change and simplification, remaining firmly committed to helping small businesses. However, each had their own agenda on the way forward and was keen to secure their own place in that future. The business support sector is itself a significant employer and holds an undeniable right and obligation to act in the best interests of it's employees, customers and where applicable, shareholders. This remains the case today. The one-stop-shop would not be a coup d'etat; this was collaboration not revolution, and the commitment of all the existing stakeholders was deemed critical to success.

The brief for the TECs was to bring together partnerships of local business support agencies and establish a single "Business Link" for advice and information. To help oil the wheels of progress, the Department of Trade and Industry committed to finance the formation of the network and to fund any resulting small business services that evolved from the process. Critical partners in each region included Chambers of Commerce, Local Authorities and Enterprise Agencies, the TEC input being to manage any resulting contract between the DTI and the Business Link. The Government believed collaboration would incorporate the strengths of each stakeholder into the new organisation. Whilst this democratic philosophy strived to achieve a sum of parts, the selected formation process would have far reaching implications in terms of consistency and quality.

The British Chambers of Commerce is a national network of independent organisations serving different regions. Enterprise agencies are also autonomous businesses serving their own locations. Clearly, each Local Authority rightly has an obligation to act in their own region's interests. Each Business Link would indeed be the sum of their stakeholders' parts, but those parts were never the same and this spawned one hundred ways to do your one-stop-shopping.

An organisational review of Business Links in 1997 concluded that these "complicated structures, with interlocking directorships, made for opaque decision-making. Moreover, the performance of the eighty nine Business Links varied considerably."[4] In an increasingly competitive business climate, it was not long before the stakeholders themselves started to question the value and character of the Business Link network, the business support giant they helped create.

Making it Happen

In 1992, the Employment Department and Department of Trade and Industry (DTI) merged, transferring responsibility for small firms to the latter. According to Lord Heseltine, the DTI "inherited a budget of some £30 million a year earmarked for this purpose. In addition we had £60 million from the DTI consultancy support schemes."[5] Business Link would replace the Department of Employment's Small Firms Service.

At that time it was rare for a Cabinet Minister to have an entrepreneurial background, more remarkable still when you consider that the Department of Trade and Industry was responsible for supporting all of the businesses in the United Kingdom. In 1957, Lord Heseltine had founded Haymarket Media Group, now one of the largest independent media companies in the UK. Lord Heseltine actively pursued his appointment as President of the Board of Trade, determined to make the one-stop-shop concept a reality and drive through an industrial policy focused on business support.

"If I have to intervene to help British companies, like the French government helps French companies, or the German government helps German companies, or the Japanese government helps Japanese companies, then I tell you, I'll intervene before breakfast, before lunch, before tea and before dinner. And I'll get up the next morning and I'll start all over again!"

Michael Heseltine MP

President of the Board of Trade

Speech from the Conservative Party Conference October 1992

The money was there to make it happen. More importantly, for the first time in history the leadership was entrepreneurial, single minded and determined.

A Friend in Need

In 1992, Lord Heseltine had a *very* simple paradigm. Small businesses wanted to concentrate on running their own businesses, not to spend time and trouble seeking out information and advice, or dealing with mountains of government paperwork. Solution? Get someone else to do it and slash government sponsored bureaucracy.

"I knew that there were very large numbers of small and medium sized enterprises out there who were running on the most rudimentary systems. They were very small and what you would effectively call one man bands, which meant that someone was doing the engineering or the selling or whatever all day, and the paperwork and management at night. If they had a problem, many of them didn't come from a background where they knew of anyone who could help them or advise them. We wanted a team of people who could hold their hand, listen to their problems, have a working knowledge of what business is about, make suggestions, ask questions and become a friend in need."

The Rt Hon the Lord Heseltine CH

Interview with author at Haymarket Media Group Head Office, Hammersmith, London

8th June, 2011

The One-Stop-Shop would be a "focal point" for accessing subsidised business advice and information. Businesses would be able to save a significant amount of time and trouble whilst someone else developed solutions and tracked down the answers. The Business Link service would be a simple way to access the best information and advice, and a catalyst for small businesses embracing external knowledge. The private consultancy sector was expected to be a key stakeholder in this strategy.

Big Bucks

Helping millions of small businesses is not cheap. The One-Stop-Shop was open to any small business in the UK. As a result an unprecedented volume of business support requests was predicted.

The network would require a robust infrastructure capable of processing such demand or risk irreparable brand damage and an early end to the project.

The Department of Trade and Industry (DTI) immediately invested £150 million to pump prime the launch of Business Link and ring fenced over £500 million for the seven years following. Access to cash would not cripple the project and this long-term financial commitment sent out a clear message of intent to stakeholders.

Changing Course

"I had long thought that the most sensible structure was to work through the Chambers of Commerce. But here we were fighting an uphill battle. With a few conspicuous exceptions, the existing chambers were no matches for their better-resourced European counterparts."

Michael Heseltine, Life in the Jungle, My Autobiography (Hodder and Stoughton 2000)

Lord Heseltine was committed to using existing provision wherever possible, and engaged the support of existing business support agencies / consultancies. However, he quickly came to the view that a "lack of coordination" between support organisations and the level of competition between them necessitated more direct action.

"We had to persuade as many local players - the Training and Enterprise Councils, the Chambers, the Local Authorities and the Enterprise Agencies to co-locate and provide a centrally managed service. From the start we received powerful support from the national umbrella organisations representing their local offspring."

Michael Heseltine, Life in the Jungle, My Autobiography (Hodder and Stoughton 2000)

In 1993, proposals for a pilot programme of Business Links were invited from interested parties. Early criticisms from stakeholders attacked the vision for being too prescriptive and too centralised in approach. These early rumblings would later become a major source of tension. By the end of that year the first pilot Business Link had been launched. The One-Stop-Shop was a reality.

Business Link would serve small and medium sized businesses for a generation.

CHAPTER TWO

BUSINESS LINK GOES NATIONAL

1994 to 1996

"Many of the old hugely labour-intensive industries are no more, right across Western Europe. By the turn of the century, perhaps half of Britain's workforce will be employed in relatively small firms. These are the new businesses on which our future jobs and prosperity will depend. We live in an increasingly knowledge-based economy. The education and skills of all our people are crucial to our prosperity and national success."

John Major MP

The Prime Minister

Competitiveness: Forging Ahead (Cm 2867). Great Britain. Dept. of Trade and Industry, Publisher HMSO, 1995

The chosen model for the Business Link was public / private sector partnership. The Department of Trade and Industry would deliver the Business Link service using a network of independent operators. These private sector partnerships were expected to work within strict brand guidelines and deliver a common suite of products and services for the small and medium sized business. The equivalent organisation in Scotland was called Scottish Business Shop. In Wales, the name was Business Connect and in Northern Ireland, the brand was the Local Enterprise Development Unit.

A generation later there is still widespread misunderstanding of the Business Link network. In part it is a success that the wider business community see Business Link as a single brand and organisation, less so that the label of "central government quango" would never quite be shaken off. Ultimately, this myth would become a commonly cited justification for the axing of Business Link.

The DTI had predicted 54 Business Links would launch by the end of 1993. Progress was slower than anticipated. On 27th September, 1993, the first Business Link was opened in Leicester. The Department of Trade and Industry had invested a not insignificant £725,000 of taxpayer cash to fund this pilot. By the end of the year a total of just three Business Links were open for business, with Birmingham and Congleton following Leicester. The Government had already invested over £3 million on the project.

Core funding from taxpayer coffers would always be important to the Business Link operators. However, the taxpayer would never be asked to cough up a 100% subsidy for Business Links. Partners would make their own contributions and each Business Link would be set income generation targets in the early years of the contracts.

From the outset, stakeholders and partners setting up Business Links were dead set against any government interference. Training and Enterprise Councils (TECs), Chambers of Commerce, Enterprise Agencies, the Confederation of British Industry and even Local Authorities were united in rejecting any central government control of their destinies. The President of the Board of Trade, Lord Heseltine, shared this insistence on retaining "local initiative, local discretion and local flexibility."[6]

TECs were promised continuity by the Department of Trade and Industry, which committed in writing to fund the development of Business Links for the first three years. Beyond that, the Government would continue to contribute funding to services on a three-year rolling programme, subject to evaluation. In financial terms this one paragraph committed over £650 million of taxpayer revenue.[7]

Going National

"Too many people were ready to accept a first stop shop approach, seeing Business Links as mere signposting agencies which left the status quo unchanged, rather than taking up the more daunting challenge of creating the consumer focused and co-located one stop shop, which was what small businesses wanted and we were determined they should have."

Michael Heseltine, Life in the Jungle, My Autobiography (Hodder and Stoughton 2000)

Building a national network of Business Links was a daunting challenge by anyone's standards. The DTI had promised to establish over 200 regional outlets by the end of 1995, run by over 80 autonomous partnerships. Half way through 1994, just 21 Business Links were open for business. Part of this delay was due to each proposal being evaluated by a National Assessment Panel, determined that successful bidders met the highest quality standards. The accreditation criteria were built squarely around a combination of the Investors in People and ISO quality standards. Achieving and retaining the ISO 9001 Quality Management Standard and Investors in People was a mandatory requirement for all Business Link Operators. Each and every partnership risked losing their three-year license if the required standards were not maintained.

The decision not to be too prescriptive in the tender was intended to keep things simple and allow flexibility. However, in reality this freedom created unforseen complexity during the bidding process. Every partnership was a unique coming together of different agencies, agendas and personalities. Moreover, the Government's preferred structure of a merged Chamber of Commerce Training and Enterprise (CCTE) was not being universally adopted. In April 1996, just six TECs and Chambers were merged.

By May 1996, a total of 79 Business Links had been established, supplying business support through 222 hub offices. Almost 5,000 businesses per week were already using the new One Stop Shops. Within just six months this figure had soared 65%.

At the end of 1996, the Government completed the national roll out of the Business Link network. In the interim, Lord Heseltine had been appointed Deputy Prime Minister and was not at the helm when his project finally came to fruition. Ultimately, a total of 89 Business Link partnerships were established to oversee 240 advice centres throughout the country. Over 100,000 small and medium sized businesses had already used the service. Usage in Birmingham alone had increased five-fold during 1996.

Setting up a national business support network is not cheap. In the 12 months to March 1995, the Department of Trade and Industry invested £13.1 million in the process, over and above partner contributions. But what exactly were the Business Links doing in return?

It's all about SME

The first hurdle for the Business Link network was to decipher exactly who the customers would be. It had already been deemed impossible to service the entire business community and like any business, the DTI decided to focus their finite resources on the customers most likely to yield highest returns. The DTI currency for return on investment was wealth creation and employment in the UK.

For the first time an agreed and shared definition of what constituted a small and medium sized business was dictated. Business Link would serve a market segment defined as 'small and medium enterprises', SME for short. This definition was a departure from traditional business definitions, which usually worked on the financial weight of an organisation. For example, the 1985 Companies Act defined a business as 'small' if sales were below £2.8 million and the workforce was less than 50 in number. For Business Link purposes the financial factor was dropped, for practical reasons as much as any other. The majority of small businesses in the UK do not have to publish full accounts in the public domain. As a result, access to reliable financial data was limited.

To automatically qualify for Business Link assistance a business needed to meet the following new criteria.

- Small business: 10 to 49 employees
- Medium business: 50 to 249 employees

This market segmentation differs from Lord Heseltine's own recollection of the Business Link vision.

"We didn't set out to serve a certain sector or a certain scale of business. We were there as a coordinated advisory business, that's what we thought the idea was, coordinating public information and giving advice about anything anyone wanted to raise, from someone who'd had some business experience. A lot of the advice I would have imagined at the early stage would have gone to people employing 2 to 5 people."

The Rt Hon the Lord Heseltine CH

Interview with author at Haymarket Media Group Head Office, Hammersmith, London

8th June, 2011

In the early years of Business Link, micro firms employing up to 9 employees were not to be discouraged. However, it is fair to say these businesses did not hear a loud knocking at their doors.

Make Way for the PBA

"We used the £90 million to offer financial help to provide business advisers, export consultants, IT specialists and design engineers."

Michael Heseltine, Life in the Jungle, My Autobiography (Hodder and Stoughton 2000)

The Personal Business Adviser (PBA) service was defined in the Business Link prospectus as a central requirement for every partnership. These advisers were to be recruited from a pool of people who had experience running businesses. Initially some Business Link Operators chose to use self-employed advisers. However, this did not prove to be popular and most opted to use directly employed staff. These "experienced" business people would take responsibility for small business problems and offer hands on support, rather than passing the buck. Furthermore, a PBA would help entrepreneurs navigate through the maze of business support, saving time and trouble by producing a tailor made list of help.

This public funded 'general practitioner' role was as revolutionary a concept as the one stop shop. It's not easy to tell a harsh truth if you need the listener to sign a cheque at the end of the day. Yet that may be *exactly* what is needed to transform a small business. For the first time small businesses could now speak to a business "expert" with nothing to sell but a frank and honest opinion, however hard that may be to hear. The PBA service description talked of wealth creation and increased employment. However, in reality the PBA mission was simply to make small and medium sized enterprises more money. Period. The rest would follow.

Seek and You Shall Find

The Business Link pilots faced similar challenges to that of any new start up business, a lack of proven credibility and customers. The early PBAs essentially started from scratch, with no client book and no customers. Networking was an essential tool of the trade in the early years. Lord Heseltine explained. "They were designed to be proactive, the front-line teams were literally going to knock on the doors of companies and say can we help?"[8]

The original target market for Business Links was small businesses with the potential to grow, usually with 10 to 249 employees. The market for Business Link advisers was then further defined. Not only must the customer be a small and medium sized enterprise, but that business must also be "growth orientated." The definition of 'growth' remains an enigma to this day. Due to this lack of clarity the PBAs would be tasked to make personal judgement calls on who they thought would be winners and losers. This individual decision making responsibility generated a degree of ambiguity and variability in the selection process.

Levering the Knowledge

In these early years of the Business Link, the PBAs had a significant degree of latitude to interpret their individual roles. However, the corporate goal had not changed. The Government still wanted the organisation to address market failure and stimulate the private consultancy market.

Business Link would send in specialist business counsellors (PBA) when companies needed in-depth assistance in a certain area. Alternatively, PBAs could decide to help companies by sourcing specialist advice from outside Business Link. It was up to them. This lack of direction effectively gave the PBA carte blanche to provide consultancy services, either free or at a cost significantly below open market rates.

Whilst not universally adopted, this freedom to consult would help alienate the business support sector for the next twenty years, fostering an "us and them" relationship for the life of the Business Link project.

If you were a consultant trying to make a living selling your knowledge, it would be difficult to sit idly by when the Government starts using tax money to effectively give away your product. In government speak they call this act "displacement." To any consultant it is called a blatant attack on their livelihood and gross interference in the free market.

Shades of Grey

"We were constantly criticised for being too prescriptive and centralised in approach. But often the moment we relaxed the broad standards we had set, local standards, far from showing the initiative about which we were so frequently told, simply relapsed to the levels we had sought to replace."

Michael Heseltine, Life in the Jungle, My Autobiography (Hodder and Stoughton 2000)

The Business Link tender process dictated a number of mandatory core services. However, the bidding partnerships were encouraged to address differing regional needs in different ways. This clause allowed freedom to innovate and be creative, but at the cost of consistency. From the outset the shared Business Link brand created an illusion that the network was a single organisation. Yet scratch beneath the surface and you would find each Business Link partnership was unique and doing things their own way. By design, the Government had inadvertently created a postcode lottery for business.

Each partnership was fulfilling the core requirement to supply information and advice (diagnosis). However, some chose to outsource services to consultants, others recruited an internal workforce. One would be focused on light touch and achieving volume engagement with small and medium sized businesses. Another would be committed to supplying "intensive assistance" and spending more time with fewer clients. The quality of recruited personnel would also be variable. One-Stop-Shop was a reality. However, a consistent offering across all the Business Links was not, and never would be.

These inherent weaknesses in the Business Link structure would be fuel on the fire for those inclined to criticise.

Whispers of Discontent

In 1996, as the Business Link network was completed, the business support sector (including a number of stakeholders in Business Link Partnerships) started to question the wisdom of the change. This ticker tape critique would be without end for the next 17 years.

During 1996, the Federation of Small Businesses (FSB) published a report claiming just 4 percent of their membership used Business Link services. Over 19,000 members had responded to the survey. Furthermore, the FSB concluded that small and medium sized businesses found the plethora of services unacceptable and confusing.

In February 1996, the Institute of Directors (IoD) published a research paper listing members' concerns about the "structure and performance" of the Business Link network. Members were worried that the declared focus on growth businesses (10 to 249 employees) might hurt smaller organisations and disadvantage start up businesses. Notably, over 80% of IOD survey respondents found the Business Link service helpful to their business (those that had actually contacted the organisation).[9] Perhaps a case of happy themselves but concerned for others?

Contrary to public opinion Business Links were actually still open to any entrepreneur (pre-start, small, medium or even large business). However, from a marketing perspective their most expensive resource (Personal Business Advisers) was deployed to help those customers with most potential. Segmenting customers and targeting finite resources on those offering highest returns is what any private sector business would and should do. In a November 1996 House of Commons debate, The Minister for Small Business, Industry and Energy Mr. Richard Page stated "I am disturbed to hear that the impression has been given that we are not there to help all businesses irrespective of size. My clear message is that Business Link is there to help any business man or woman, irrespective of the size of company, because from little acorns grow the big oak trees."

Hard to argue with the acorn analogy, but this policy confirmed the actual target market was anyone, anywhere. Everyone in the UK paying tax had already contributed to the Business Link service. Being able to say "no", one of the most important controls for steering and managing a successful organisation, was no longer an option for the partnerships. The floodgates had been opened.

The whispers of discontent from the business support sector would build over the next 20 years, sometimes with justification and always with the interests of their stakeholders at heart. Ultimately, these voices became a powerful lobby for change and effectively sealed the demise of Business Link.

Building Business As Usual

The Business Link network was built. Lord Heseltine had stated prior to his departure from the DTI that after such "rapid expansion, the watchwords (for Business Link) should be stability and solid professional management of the network, not gimmickry."[10] The 89 new Business Link partnerships no doubt shared this opinion. However, despite the firm financial commitment from the DTI, a caveat had been attached. Within five years of launch each individual Business Link partnership must generate at least 25% of its income from outside central government. The DTI suggested the most likely source of alternative revenue would be the end consumers, small and medium sized businesses.

Faced with this financial challenge, a plethora of income generating ideas spawned from the within the Business Link network. Each region sought to expand their core service, identify alternative European funded initiatives and raise private revenue. Each Business Link partnership approached the challenge in different ways. For example Business Link Norfolk and Waveney shunned a direct charging structure from the start, choosing instead to win other public funded projects and integrate these into their flavour of the Business Link offer. In contrast, less than 100 miles to the west the partnership in Hertfordshire had a charging policy from the start, going on to form one of the most commercial Business Link brands, and incidentally best performing. This business model would earn grudging respect from their peers.

The charging policy, and resulting cultural implications, formed the most visible differences between each Business Link partnership. It was also the main source of uneasiness within the Business Link network. Could a government-funded initiative really claim to be impartial if a sales agenda was on the table? Even more anxiety and protest originated from the consultancy sector itself. How could Business Link activity stimulate the market if the "honest brokers" kept all the best customers for themselves? A need for payment muddied the waters for everyone.

Business Link was now a single brand offering 89 different experiences for small and medium sized businesses. This effect was amplified further by differences in quality and personality of the individual Business Advisers. After all, business advice in the mid-nineties was a people to people process, not a fistful of email.

Despite these challenges for the future, in the there and now the initial impact of the Business Link network was impressive. Research for the last quarter of 1996 showed some 8,250 businesses a week were already using Business Link services. Founder Lord Heseltine was clearly satisfied with the pace of progress. "There's a very real demand out there and the reputation of Business Link is growing."[11]

Second Phase Thinking

In 1996, not one to sit on their laurels, the Department of Trade and Industry immediately sought to improve the performance and capability of the Business Link network (particularly as tax expenditure must be always be justified to Commons Committees).

A pilot project involving 20 Business Link Innovation and Technology Counsellors was underway. Design, intellectual property and applications engineering were seen as critical for the increasingly knowledge based economy.

In addition, the brokerage service to consultants now came under closer scrutiny, in a bid to raise quality standards. An approved supplier list for Business Link customers was an inevitable outcome. Despite significant future investment, the majority of consultants (and indeed the Personal Business Advisers themselves) would never fully embrace a national suppliers register. As a result of this lack of transparency and information trail, the income targeted Business Links would always be open to accusations of "black book" business and bias.

In other areas, the Business Link strategy was already being altered. The Government understandably wanted to see a return on investment in terms of economic growth. As a result, a number of sectors were discouraged, if not formally, then certainly informally. Retail was perceived to add least value to each region, as this sector was assumed to be re-circulating money in the local area, rather than attracting inward investment from outside (despite being one of the largest employers). If you were one of the tens of thousands of small businesses retailing goods, then you were not in the Business Link target market. Whilst probably right from an economic perspective, this decision was difficult to explain when a retailer was on the end of the phone asking for help.

A series of shared performance indicators for each Business Link partnership were in place. These included number of new start-ups, survival rates, employment levels and at the core of every future evaluation of Business Link – gross value added in financial terms. Measurement was light touch in the infancy of the Business Link network, but in the new millennium demands for proof of worth would seriously increase the burden of administration and put pressure on an already stretched service.

In 1996, these were arguments for the future. On the face of it, all seemed well with the Business Link strategy. An Ernst & Young study concluded any Business Link teething troubles had been "associated with the development phase rather than being intrinsic to the model."[12]

The Business Link One-Stop-Shop had arrived and was here to stay.

CHAPTER THREE

A TOOLKIT OF COMPETITIVENESS

"Every company will have a local point of access to a wide range of services, which Personal Business Advisers will put together and tailor to its needs. They will take responsibility for giving advice on customers' problems, not just refer them on to someone else if they do not have an immediate answer. The new Personal Business Adviser service is central to Business Links."

Helping Business To Win: DTI Competitiveness White Paper 1994

By the end of 1995, the Business Link project had a broad vision for the future of business and real live people on the ground. It was time to decide what to do with them. The One Stop Shop concept was designed to simplify access to business support and was about to be beefed up with a suitcase of DTI sponsored products. Once again the Government was reluctant to be too prescriptive, keen to allow each region's Business Link an opportunity to tailor their support to local needs. However, the Government did dictate some areas of universal practice. Each Business Link Operator (BLO) was compelled to deliver the following common suite of products and services.

- Personal Business Advisers to work with a business over a period to diagnose the needs of each customer and tailor support accordingly.
- Information and advice on:
    o Business strategy and change
    o Financial management, late payment, taxation and grants
    o Regulatory requirements
    o The Single Market
    o Training and development
    o Business start-up
    o Other business information, and databases
- Export services
- Consultancy
- Innovation, quality, design and technology services
- Awareness events
- Training courses

The Department of Trade and Industry developed and supplied a central portfolio of support material in an effort to achieve a degree of standardisation and consistency across the network. This offering would be widely known as the Information, Diagnostic and Brokerage model (IDB) and remained the main delivery tool for the life of Business Link. The service offering in individual regions still varied depending on the amount of focus Partnerships chose to put on each element - information, diagnosis or brokerage. Business Links strived to give advisers the tools needed to create change in business performance. A number of these initiatives were already in existence and were welcomed into the Business Link organisation.

Express Train

"An enterprising business will recognise and invest in the potential of its people. Success needs people of high calibre, working well as teams. But it is the personal qualities of the prime movers in an organisation that largely determine that success. This is particularly so for the small firm, where the vision and will to succeed are often in the hands of one or two people with little or none of the back-up of larger organisations."

Creating the Enterprise Centre of Europe
DTI Competitiveness White Paper 1996

The Government of the day believed small businesses neglected investment in training and skills, faced with the day-to-day pressure of trading and perceived prohibitive costs. Therefore, Business Links integrated training advice into the other services on offer.

Prior to the formation of Business Link, Training and Enterprise Councils (TEC) and Investors in People UK (IiP) had made good progress in improving attitudes to training. The IiP framework is a step-by-step process to develop a growth strategy founded on the capabilities of people (employees). The product is deliberately non-prescriptive to make it easier for small businesses to manage. Indeed, it is possible for an IiP adviser to coach customers without pen or paper, as non-prescriptive as you can get.

Where appropriate, a Personal Business Adviser could broker in TEC support (subsidised training etc.) and the Investors in People standard to address skill gaps in small businesses.

Willingness to Compare

"Competitiveness is not just a challenge for Government and for business. It requires a change in behaviour by all of us; an openness to new ideas and above all, a willingness to compare ourselves with the best in the world; to face up to how well we are doing and if the answer is not favourable, to do something about it."

John Major MP

Prime Minister – Foreword. Creating the Enterprise Centre of Europe

DTI Competitiveness White Paper 1996

The Department of Trade and Industry (DTI) was adamant that if small and medium sized businesses were to grow, they must measure and compare. Indeed this was the precise approach adopted by the Government (on an International scale) when they created the Competitiveness programme.

Since 1989 the DTI had funded the "Managing in the 90s" programme, which promoted best practice in smaller firms through over 3,300 events and attracted more than 100,000 participants. Despite this success, a key catalyst for the formation of Business Link had been an apparent reluctance on the part of small and medium sized businesses to look outside their own organisation. Businesses were assumed to be fixated on their own actions to survive and prosper, rather than how other people were doing. In 1995, the "Small Firms Survey: Competitiveness" (ABCC and Alex Lawrie) found that just 21% of small businesses were using any form of benchmarking.

This lack of activity was due in part to the drought of relevant benchmark data, against which small businesses could compare. When Business Link launched, the Personal Business Advisers had to rely on old school methods to benchmark customers, purchasing competitor accounts, setting up collaborative visits (you show me yours and I'll show you mine) and trying to make sense of more general data available in market research reports. This market failure drove the creation of a National Benchmark Index.

<u>Winning Moves</u>

Faced with a black hole of benchmark data and no sign of the private sector filling this competitiveness gap, the Government acted. Their vision was to create a "comprehensive National Benchmarking Network, which should help many more firms to exploit this effective route to achieving world class standards."[13]

In 1996, the DTI engaged the private sector company Winning Moves to deliver the Connect Best Practice programme, which was subsequently followed in 1998 by a £9 million contract to develop and manage a National Benchmark Index for the next decade.

When conceived, it was envisaged Business Link advisers and other agencies would help at least 10,000 small to medium sized businesses access the National Benchmark Index each year. The expected return on this investment for the taxpayer was estimated to be a combined increase in profits of £8 million per annum for the small and medium sized business sector.

<u>You Show Me Yours; I'll Show You Mine</u>

The Benchmark Index allowed customers to assess their own performance (financial and otherwise) using a set of key measures.

The DTI wanted to create a national benchmark tool for small businesses. The vision was for an IT based system, to be used by entrepreneurs who wanted to compare their business performance against thousands of other organisations, in key areas such as finance and operations.

Comparison would always have limitations, as no two businesses are exactly the same. However, if the findings were interpreted well by an entrepreneur (assisted by the Business Link Adviser), the Benchmark Index could focus in on weaknesses and strengths, not in isolation, but within the peer group of a business. Benchmarking compared an organisation against their competition and produced a relative performance score. A small business may be pleased with an 80% efficiency rate, but if all their competitors score 90%, far from being top of the pile they are a poor performer. Benchmarking would never be an exact science. However, in this respect, if a big enough sample of relevant quality data was available, the difference it could make to a small business was significant.

Unfortunately, it was a chicken and egg scenario. Small businesses would only invest valuable time to submit a benchmark data set if they could see value in the process. Yet this value was directly linked to the number of data sets available for comparison. A carrot was needed for small businesses to invest their time. Therefore, the DTI offered grant funding for each completed submission of data. This money was a significant incentive to use the Index for both small businesses (subsidised consultancy) and Business Link advisers (easy to please clients). Within a short time frame the pump-primed initiative had collected enough small business benchmark data to claim "the largest service of its type in the world" (albeit there wasn't much competition to speak of in the first place).

Initial feedback from Benchmark Index users suggested 70 percent of medium sized businesses acted on the results. Equally as significant, more small and medium sized businesses were now measuring their *own* performance in a systematic and structured way, which they could review year on year. Keeping an eye on the competition was helpful; monitoring your own progress and improvement was critical to remain competitive. A "measure to win" culture was growing.

Cash Points

A small business can have the best business plan, a great product idea and the brains of Britain, but if there is no cash for investment it's just a fiction. The finance issue was central to the Personal Business Adviser service, particularly when one of their primary purposes was to lever in knowledge from the paid consultant sector. Whatever the economic climate, small and medium sized businesses struggle to secure finance for growth. The risk to reward ratio just doesn't offer enough return for most financiers. Sounds like a 'market failure', time for some government intervention.

Bankrolling the Banker

The Business Link toolkit would contain a number of government sponsored higher risk lending initiatives, the existing Small Firms Loan Guarantee Scheme (SFLG) being the flagship product. SFLG was launched in 1981, and at the risk of over simplifying, the Government promised the banks they would cover up to 80% of their losses if you ran off to Acapulco. Thus banks were being encouraged to give loans to small businesses that would usually fail to satisfy lenders' requirements for collateral and / or track record.

In September 1996, the Government further enhanced the SFLG. Now the scheme was open to even smaller businesses, specialist lenders (technology) were brought on board and the maximum payback period increased from seven to ten years. Yet some banks still didn't play ball, a bad investment is a bad investment, losing 20% was worse than keeping your money tucked up safely in bed each night.

After the launch of Business Link, take up of the scheme increased from £52 million in 1992-93 to £240 million in 1995. In return, banks were asked to refer their customers to Business Links. These relationships with banks would always be patchy, although there were undoubtedly pockets of success in a few regions.

A Host of Angels

In the mid-nineties equity investment in small and medium sized businesses was unregulated and perceived to be the domain of larger organisations. The Government committed to raising awareness of this type of finance, creating a national Business Angels network. Business Link advisers could now introduce small and medium sized businesses of any size to a group of equity investors. Entrepreneurs could sell shares in their organisation in return for sizeable cash injections and with a bit of luck, some added expertise. However, only the very best small and medium sized business propositions were successful. The percentage of pitches through Business Link that secured an equity partner would be in the low single digits, mirroring the success rate of the equity investment sector in general.

Money for Nothing

Contrary to popular belief, Business Link was never a grants factory. Each Business Link partnership had a clear brief to target growth potential entrepreneurs in small and medium sized businesses. The Personal Business Advisers had a responsibility to know where and how to access grant support, if available. However, if a small business just wanted to know about grant money and was not open to external input, then they would be told the answer to their question and politely moved on.

Grant funding for the small and medium sized businesses rarely exceeded £5,000, was often a "match" deal requiring the business to invest half the amount, involved a fair bit of paperwork and was always linked to a specific growth project. Goody bags of cash were not being stored in the back office.

Over the years the Department of Trade and Industry would add a number of grant schemes to the toolkit, including Grant for Business Investment (capital), SMART awards (innovation) and awards through the later Benchmark Index Scheme (consultancy). As a result, an increasing number of small and medium sized businesses engaged private sector consultancy. Measuring the results and quality of the resulting transfer of knowledge was more challenging.

Availability of grant funding would never meet the expectation of free money created by government initiatives in the early nineties. This expectation would continue long after the grants dried up. Yes, the Personal Business Adviser had a responsibility to source funding wherever possible, but not at the detriment of the advice itself. A small but vocal section of the market remained incensed that their apparent 'Government given right' to free cash was being blighted, apparently personally by Business Link. It was not uncommon for grant chasers to be so desperate for cash that they became understandably blind to the idea that other advice might help. The harsh reality in terms of Business Link strategy is these people would be unlikely to contribute to the growth of the economy.

Financially challenged customers would become a continuous thorn in the side for Business link Operators trying to hit a 90% plus satisfaction target. If a small business thinks you are withholding a bag of cash, and doesn't want your help anyway, better strike that down as an unhappy face.

Export Not Import

At the end of 1996, Business Link had already appointed over 50 Export counsellors. These specialist advisers had been recruited from the private sector in a bid to promote export as a viable business opportunity for small businesses.

At this early stage Export Counsellors focused entirely on promoting outward sales to other countries, rather than import opportunities. This policy supported the Government's agenda to increase the number of organisations selling goods internationally. It was less helpful to an ever-increasing number of small and medium sized businesses trying to buy materials and goods more cheaply overseas. Keeping costs to a minimum in a bid to stay competitive was always a priority. Despite this policy, most advisers would agree to help with import when asked. The vast majority of advisers always had the best interests of clients at heart.

The Export Counsellors were a powerful addition to the Business Link offering. International trade is an ever-present, albeit often missed opportunity for almost every small to medium sized business. The Export Counsellor tool kit included a substantial list of DTI subsidised products, including sourcing market research, and linking up businesses with contacts in overseas countries. In 1996, the DTI pledged to invest an additional £30 million over four years to help entrepreneurs attend Trade Fairs and Inward / Outward Missions. Their remit was simple, help small businesses navigate through the inherent bureaucracy of selling abroad and get them exporting.

The importance of export to the United Kingdom was clear to all some twenty years later when, despite sweeping cuts in public sector funding, the coalition Government ring-fenced funding for international trade. The UK Trade and Investment (UKTI) advisory service outlived the Business Link network.

Rules and Tribulations

"Rules can act as a deterrent to market entry, unnecessary requirements impose costs on business, and the burden of official forms and paperwork wastes management time. Bad regulation stands in the way of innovation, investment and jobs."

Forging Ahead – Competitiveness Government White Paper 1995

By the nineties, the burden of red tape and regulations was already a concern for all businesses. Legal compliance is ever present in the list of threats to a business, albeit the topic would never be one to get the juices, or finances, flowing (not in the right direction anyway!). Business Link partnerships had a responsibility to ensure their customers complied with the law and regulatory requirements. Unfortunately Business Link advisers did not have a brief or the qualifications to give legal advice. Yet common compliance legislation such as Health and Safety at Work Act (1974) demanded just that detailed level of knowledge. The consequences of being non-compliant could be extremely serious to both a business and their personnel. As a result the Personal Business Advisers were trained to have a working knowledge of regulatory requirements and enough know-how to recognise the risks and symptoms of impending disaster (financial or otherwise). Ultimately, compliance with regulations remained the responsibility of the small and medium sized business, and the toolkit relied heavily on information leaflets (DIY) and brokered in fee earning legal advisers.

In 1996, progress on deregulation was a government priority, rather than a reality.

Innovation Nation

The Competitiveness agenda believed innovation was a critical skill needed by small and medium sized businesses of the future.

The Innovation and Technology Counsellor (ITC) was conceived to drive this activity at the coalface. These specialist advisers provided guidance on intellectual property issues and design. Another important element of their role was to be a link between small businesses and Universities, research bodies and other centres of knowledge transfer. The ITC would also seek out funding for resulting projects using specialist grants wherever possible.

The ITC needed an in-depth knowledge of design, new product development and intellectual property protection. A wide active network of contacts in the technology sector was also vital. To support this activity the DTI established the Supernet, a cluster of technological experts accessible via the Business Link network.

In 1996, the Business Links could claim national coverage for the ITC team, at an estimated cost of £4.3 million per annum.

Revolting Consulting

A perceived market failure in the consultancy sector had already given birth to the Business Link. Culturally the Government believed a typical small to medium sized business was just too suspicious of the value on offer, or just had no idea where to start.

The Government believed the consultancy sector lacked regulation and leadership, delivered too much duplication, appeared inconsistent regarding quality and most seriously of all, was too narrow in scope to meet the demands of small and medium sized organisations. In their defence, consultants understandably focused on developing products to meet the needs of larger businesses with larger pockets. If the consultancy sector was truly this fragmented, Business Link should have been the perfect bedfellow to stimulate the market. A national team of paid for sales people willing to go and get new work for consultants, opening up the untapped small business market. Yet the reality was very different, as the vast majority of consultants remained highly suspicious of the Personal Business Advisers who they all too readily assumed were a blockage rather than a pipeline to new customers.

Grant funding to help customers pay prices was fine for consultants. A lot more difficult to swallow was having a Personal Business Adviser monitor their project, advising the client along the way and generally sticking a nose in to make sure it worked. Small businesses didn't care about all this politicking. But they did care about value for money and return on investment. Personal Business Advisers would stimulate the market, but there would be no easy rides for any supplier working for a Business Link customer. If a consultant did not have the ability to really make a difference, they would be quickly exposed. It wasn't long before both sides were complaining, the Personal Business Advisers about the quality of the consultants, and the consultants about the quality / lack of referrals.

The first of a number of national consultants registers was conceived to bridge this lack of trust. Rather than nurture relationships between all the parties involved, the Government effectively removed the Consultant and Personal Business Adviser from the decision making process. Consultants had to meet a minimum set of standards to be included on this supplier list (for a fee initially). Business Link advisers were forced to use only suppliers listed on the approved database of providers. This policy would be sacrosanct on future grant schemes. If selected consultants were not on the list, no money.

Little account was taken of the key ingredients in a consultancy transaction – people. Yes, if you remove people from the process it reduces risk of bias and corruption, but at what cost? Ideally small businesses want to work with someone they can get along with (now and in the future), people who can inject the right knowledge at the best price and won't try to deceive or exploit. Appointing a consultant could be the most important decision a business ever takes. Bringing in external people is drenched in both risk and reward potential. The Personal Business Adviser helped customers find a best match, policing the transaction for the benefit of both parties. The customer was more confident to buy. The consultant was encouraged to deliver optimum value and, as a result, won a powerful advocate in their new customer.

Regrettably, in general the consultancy sector never signed up on the approved lists in great numbers. It is worth observing that, in the absence of any grant incentives, if a consultant was high quality and successful why would they jump through hoops to get to a small to medium sized business (with a correspondingly sized wallet)?

The majority of Business Link Advisers always first acted in the interests of the small to medium sized business customer. As a result, if suppliers on an approved list could not fill the need, the Business Adviser would seek out consultants that would. The consultancy sector was receiving a continuous market stimulus, just not in a transparent and 'equal shares for all' way. Most Business Link Advisers never knowingly abused this impartial aspect of their role. Providing a customer with a choice of three suppliers was always a strict Business Link policy, mitigating bias. This off-radar activity became an issue later when the value of Business Link was challenged. Increasing the take up of consultancy was a key objective for Business Link. However, the number of recorded market transactions by small and medium sized businesses created a perception of failure. If the activity had not been strictly and religiously recorded, what other conclusion could be reached?

In the future many would cite this apparent lack of brokerage activity as rationale for closing Business Link. Business Link advisers were labeled civil servants who signposted onto others to do the work, an unnecessary link in the chain. A thoroughly misinformed view, albeit understandable based on the available data.

The Government obsession for a quality-approved supplier list continued to the very end of the Business Link advisory service.

Quality Street

"When products and services meet our expectations, we tend to take this for granted and be unaware of the role of standards. However, when standards are absent, we soon notice. We soon care when products turn out to be of poor quality, do not fit, are incompatible with equipment that we already have, are unreliable or dangerous."

International Organization for Standardization (ISO) 2011

Best practice was further encouraged in small businesses by actively promoting the long established ISO family of quality standards. The International Organization for Standardization had been founded in 1947. Their ISO 9000:1994 quality model was a paper-based system to promote quality in design, development, production, installation and servicing. Preventive action was at the core of the Standard.

In simple terms the final documentation set out the way things were done in an organisation, drilled down into the critical processes and implemented checks and measures to ensure the final outputs met expectations. The setting up of this management tool would almost always require knowledge of a paid consultant, a requisite to becoming ISO accredited by the governing body.

Businesses often interpreted the need to monitor and evaluate literally and ended up creating a mini-library of process manuals. In these situations any potential value was strangled by design, unmanageable due to a self-engineered administration overload. Like any document based system to improve business, the devil was in the detail and having the right consultant to implement the process was critical.

The Government of the day recognised that certification could be "burdensome for small firms" and set out to encourage bodies and consultants to be sensitive to the needs of these organisations. Successfully too, as a series of tailored standards were introduced. Additional guidance for small and medium sized businesses planning to use ISO was published by the DTI.

The Personal Business Adviser was trained to recognise opportunities for improvement, supply guidance and lever in the *right* consultant for the customer.

And finally...

The Personal Business Adviser (PBA) threw their brain into the toolkit. If you were a small business, the Business Link adviser delivered an honest, unemotional and impartial appraisal on performance. A stop and think slap in the business face.

If it was right for a business and could improve performance, the PBA was not afraid to raise uncomfortable truths or hold up a mirror. What was the entrepreneur going to do, withhold the non-existent payment? However, these business issues can be explosive both emotionally and commercially, so diplomacy and communication were core skills needed to successfully deliver this level of honesty. In the majority of cases, the small to medium sized business was drawn out of their comfort zone for the first time and this generated respect rather than angst.

Furthermore, if needed, a small business was able to draw on the opinions of an entire team of Personal Business Advisers. An all-team email or casebook meeting could submit a business model and strategy to over twenty sets of business eyes. At its best the Personal Business Adviser team subjected business strategies to a unique and extreme stress test, giving small and medium sized businesses the confidence to act and invest in growth.

Chasing the World Class Company

The Personal Business Adviser toolkit would remain pretty much unchanged for the next twenty years. New initiatives would come and go, sometimes the names would change, but essentially the package of support remained the same.

A small to medium sized business entrepreneur could access as much or as little of Business Link as they saw fit. If you were an entrepreneur and never used the Business Link service, consider that tens of thousands of businesses were using Personal Business Advisers each year. Competitors, suppliers and customers were taking full advantage of this on tap knowledge giveaway.

A public financed advisory service on this scale did not come cheap. In 2010, Secretary of State for Business, Innovation and Skills, Mark Prisk MP, confirmed the cost of employing and training Personal Business Advisers that year alone was £55.95 million excluding expenses and overheads.[14]

In a credit crunched economy, *personal* business advice was doomed.

CHAPTER FOUR

THE KNOWLEDGE DRIVEN ECONOMY

1997 to 1998

"The modern world is swept by change. This new world challenges business to be innovative and creative, to improve performance continuously, to build new alliances and ventures. But it also challenges Government: to create and execute a new approach to industrial policy.

Old fashioned state intervention did *not* and cannot work."

The Rt Hon Tony Blair MP
Prime Minister
Our Competitive Future Building the Knowledge Driven Economy December 1998

On 2nd May, 1997, less than a year since construction of the Business Link network was finished, Tony Blair and his New Labour party swept to power in a landslide election victory. Lord Heseltine had left the post of President of the Board of Trade on 5th July, 1995, to become Deputy Prime Minister. His successor Ian Lang stuck to the departing Lord Heseltine's watchwords for Business Link - "stability and solid professional management of the network, not gimmickry." [15] New Labour would steer Business Link in new directions.

Reform Becomes the Norm

Whilst each party made noises about supporting small business in their manifestos, the Labour Party was the only one to expressly commit to changing Business Link.

"Support for small businesses will have a major role in our plans for economic growth. We will cut unnecessary red tape; provide for statutory interest on late payment of debts; improve support for high-tech start-ups; improve the quality and relevance of advice and training through a reformed Business Links network and the University for Industry; and assist firms to enter overseas markets more effectively."

New Labour, New Life For Britain – Labour Party Manifesto 1996

(The Liberal Democrat 1997 manifesto stated a desire to integrate the organisation into a merger with other business support organisations, overseen by a Regional Development Agency, rather than expressly make changes to the service).

Yet the concept of the one-stop-shop for small and medium sized businesses still received broad cross party support. Any agenda for change would be an "enhancement", rather than a torched earth policy. Unsurprisingly, whilst the Labour Party supported the Business Link concept, the left of centre had issues with the right, particularly over some of the claims on progress. The Labour 1997 manifesto disputed the positive impact on small businesses, claiming instead that over "half a million small employers" had vanished since 1990. A number of Labour Ministers expressed publicly their dissatisfaction with how the Conservative Party handled Business Link.

"I think it had been set up far too rapidly and not piloted properly but, having said that, I think there was and there is some tremendously good work that has been done in the Business Link Network and I am constantly impressed to listen to small businesses about the help and support and advice that they have had from the network."

Barbara Roche MP Parliamentary Under-Secretary of State for Small Firms, Trade & Industry (1997)

Contrast this grudging acknowledgement with the rather more forthright statement in 2003 from Patricia Hewitt, the renamed Secretary of State for Trade and Industry, who told Parliament – "Business Link, which was started by the Conservatives, was in a pretty pathetic state when we took over, and there were many complaints from customers." Five years is clearly a long time in politics and business support.

In a 2011 interview with the author, Lord Heseltine disputed this accusation out of hand. "My information is that we got a lot of enquiries, there was a demand and I personally never saw any serious complaints. I heard about press criticism but I've long since learned to discount press criticism. You have to aim off for that sort of selective reporting."

21st Century Business

On the 8th October, 1997, the Labour Government published "Enhanced Business Links - a Vision for the 21st Century." This modest mission statement would be the catalyst for a seismic shift (albeit fairly subtle) in the value offered to small and medium sized businesses.

Barbara Roche MP, Parliamentary Under-Secretary of State for Small Firms, Trade & Industry presented this statement of intent to Parliament.

"A good deal of the previous Government's vision for Business Links was concerned with issues of organisation and structure. My vision for an enhanced Business Link service is about quality and about service, about continuous improvement and excellence, about focusing on your needs as a customer first, last, and always."

Barbara Roche MP. Parliamentary Under-Secretary of State for Small Firms, Trade & Industry

Enhanced Business Links - a Vision for the 21st Century

Dept. of Trade and Industry Great Britain (1997)

Sounds like the usual hoopla and lip service on the face of it, but yet again the devil was in the detail. Labour would instigate a campaign of rationalisation, re-engineering both delivery and value available to small businesses.

The statement also set out a longer-term commitment to reorganise the way Business Link partnerships were managed. In the future "regionally-based Development Agencies" would be tasked to "build new partnerships between small businesses, local Councils, Business Links, TECs and local Chambers of Commerce." In the new millennium this prophecy would eventually lead to the DTI relinquishing control of the Business Link network to the regions. The single brand approach would continue to serve its purpose and the vast majority of small and medium sized businesses would remain oblivious to these changes (and their related cost).

Rightly, most small business entrepreneurs were more concerned with what Business Link could do for *them* personally, in the there and now. The majority of small businesses judged the service in micro not macro terms i.e. their own personal experience of using the service and the resulting impact on their bottom line, not the general economy.

One Stop Rot

Barbara Roche MP reported that there was "still confusion where to go and who to talk to, in order to get the help you need." The full Business Link network had been in place less than a year. It was facing a huge challenge to get four million business owners to hear their message, especially when e-communication was still in its infancy. Whether quick to judge or not, there is little doubt a large number of businesses remained confused. In the future each and every review of Business Link performance would reaffirm this failure to communicate.

In 1992, it was estimated that over 2,000 different business support initiatives were running in England. Repeated government attempts to rationalise the number of schemes in the business support landscape had failed. With so many stakeholder interests in play, simplification was continuously thwarted by a complex and fast changing market. Indeed, one of the rationales to appoint Personal Business Advisers in the first place had been to accept this complexity as fact in the sector. The Business Link adviser navigated through the maze. If you were a small business customer, it was their responsibility to know the roads to business support and be the well-travelled guide to relevant support. Barbara Roche was damning.

"I want this to develop further so that in every case the Business Link partnership provides a one-stop shop, which is a reality and not an empty slogan."

Barbara Roche MP. Parliamentary Under-Secretary of State for Small Firms, Trade & Industry

Enhanced Business Links - a Vision for the 21st Century

Dept. of Trade and Industry Great Britain (1997)

By the late nineties, this new one stop shop vision translated into a merger process that reduced the number of Business Link partnerships by 50%. Fewer partnerships would create larger organisations serving wider regions. Incorporating more stakeholders and reducing competition between the partners would create a more integrated, efficient and simple beast. That was the theory anyway.

The success of this approach was measured by brand awareness and attrition of the service. Growth in these performance indicators would be impressive, thanks in no small part to a sustained and significant investment of taxpayer funds on advertising.

Fitness Trainer

Margaret Beckett MP, President of the Board of Trade (2 May 1997 to 27 July 1998) was keen to get cracking and promised to develop "the most successful and fastest growing SME sector in the world." Her vision was to create "within five years":

- More small firms growing into bigger businesses

- More small and medium sized businesses in global markets

- More businesses engaged in electronic commerce

- More small businesses becoming learning organisations

- More small and medium sized businesses exploiting technology

No prizes for guessing the word of the day – MORE. Margaret Beckett wanted more bang for the government buck from Business Link. Once again, Personal Business Advisers were deemed integral to realising the vision. The first target for "enhancement" was a perceived lack of quality in the Business Link service. As we know, not everyone in the business support sector was spinning cartwheels to see a government funded advisory service on the march in their own backyard, whatever the positive pretence.

"Business Links will provide crucial support to the SME sector. They will provide a small army of personal fitness trainers for businesses - helping you to get into shape to meet the challenges and seize the opportunities of the 21st century."

Margaret Beckett MP President of the Board of Trade

Enhanced Business Links - a Vision for the 21st Century

Dept. of Trade and Industry Great Britain (1997)

The Labour Party was concerned that "in too many areas small to medium sized businesses were still suspicious about the quality of service on offer." Not surprisingly, the Personal Business Adviser team became increasingly under the spotlight.

Tony Blair and the Drive for Knowledge

Less than a year after the publication of "Enhanced Business Links" the Government released the fourth and most influential Competitiveness White paper, "Our Competitive Future - Building the Knowledge Driven Economy" (December 1998). New Labour believed relying just on nuts and bolts business advice was no longer fit for purpose in the modern economy. Small and medium sized businesses had to change their whole philosophy to keep the country competitive.

"Our success depends on how well we exploit our most valuable assets: our knowledge, skills, and creativity. In Government, in business, in our universities and throughout society we must do much more to foster a new entrepreneurial spirit: equipping ourselves for the long term, prepared to seize opportunities, committed to constant innovation and enhanced performance."

The Rt Hon Tony Blair MP - Prime Minister

Our Competitive Future: Building the Knowledge Driven Economy (Cm. 4167)

Great Britain. Dept. of Trade & Industry (December 1998)

If you were a small business entrepreneur, *you* were now the main barrier to competitiveness. For the first time the finger had been pointed straight at the entrepreneurial ability of business leaders. The DTI would tackle this deficiency by addressing personal weakness first, nuts and bolts capability second.

In World Class Company

"We also need entrepreneurial individuals with the vision to turn new ideas into winning products and processes. Entrepreneurship is the lifeblood of the new British economy, in large companies as well as small. We will encourage a new generation of entrepreneurs, who will create the businesses on which our future prosperity will depend."

Our Competitive Future: Building the Knowledge Driven Economy (Cm 4167.)

Great Britain. Dept. of Trade & Industry (December 1998)

In business the concept of being "world class" is long established and even longer studied. World-class theory directly related performance to management capability.

In 1994, the DTI and Confederation of British Industry completed a study of 120 of the most successful businesses in the United Kingdom. The resulting "Winning Report" set out a DNA blueprint of entrepreneurial traits found within every world-class company.[16] Their findings affirmed that the world-class entrepreneur:

- Champions change

- Continuously sets and pursues growth targets

- Adopts an open approach to customers, employees and suppliers

- Unlocks the potential of their people

- Develops skills and encourages team working

- Constantly learns from others and is open to new ideas

- Innovates and continuously seeks to introduce new products

- Repeatedly strives to exploit new technology

- Anticipates the needs of their customers

- Continuously drives to exceed customer expectations

The World Class entrepreneur did not pursue each goal in isolation, but rather had a holistic approach (instinctive even) to enterprise, making sure each activity boosted another. For example, training staff would be a catalyst for new thinking, increasing levels of innovation, generating new products and delighting customers.

Most significantly to the future anatomy of business support, the Winning Report concluded that size of business was not a determinant of success. Whatever the scale of your business, adopting World Class thinking could create a step change result. However, entrepreneurs in small and medium sized organisations faced sustained attacks on their ability to manage i.e. lack of time, ability and focus to make World Class happen. The Government planned to tackle these weaknesses head on.

The Winning Report found that "of hyper-growth companies (those which have doubled both turnover and employees over three years), 54% integrate activities with larger companies, compared with 40% of lower-performing firms. Almost 50% use technology transfer networks to gain access to new technology, compared with 28% of slower-growing companies. However, overall SMEs usually go it alone." The Government was determined small businesses of the future should break out of their comfort zone, make some business friends, expand their horizons and look to collaborate. The Knowledge Economy White Paper called for businesses to work together, to exchange best practice and embrace peer-to-peer learning. Facilitating this type of relationship was not only seen as economically beneficial for the small and medium sized business, but also one of the most effective methods for transferring knowledge. In the new future, Business Links would be expected to facilitate action, rather than be a "hands on" solver of your problems. It was hoped the private sector would do the rest.

Your traits in 98

In 1998, the Knowledge Economy White Paper predicted a number of threats to business over the next decade. Low cost economies would grow by exploiting "new technologies, skilled people and mobile capital." The forming global economy would enable a rapid exchange of knowledge, spreading innovative products, processes and services. Electronic commerce would change the way business met the demands of their customers. New technologies, science and knowledge would be the corner stones of competitiveness. Competition no longer came solely from the neighbour's backyard, but from anywhere in the world.

The message was clear. If you were a small business you could no longer live inside a business bubble. The Government wanted you to break out of your comfort zone, to "identify, capture and market the knowledge base", using technological knowledge in our Universities and research organisations to generate profit.

"The UK's distinctive capabilities are not raw materials, land or cheap labour. They must be our knowledge, skills and creativity."

Our Competitive Future: Building the Knowledge Driven Economy (Cm. 4167)
Great Britain. Dept. of Trade & Industry (December 1998)

Long-term success could only be achieved by exploiting capabilities which competitors find hard to imitate. Making that happen would be the responsibility of small and medium sized businesses. Never fear though, the DTI promised to help you by fostering entrepreneur skills in schools and Universities, creating a new £150 million Enterprise Fund just for small and medium sized businesses and delivering a "new Business Link service providing advice to 10,000 innovative start-ups with growth potential each year."

Small businesses were being told, if you fail to prepare "a greater understanding of risk and business management skills", then prepare to fail.

The New You

The Knowledge Driven Economy paper mapped out exactly how small businesses must reengineer their business DNA to prosper, to become "vigorous" entrepreneurs. Business leaders of the future must have an insatiable hunger for learning throughout their organisation and the ability to recognise commercial opportunity, wherever and whenever it may reveal itself. Yet skills alone were not enough for the Government.

Building the Knowledge Driven Economy

The modern world is swept by change. New technologies emerge constantly, new markets are opening up. There are new competitors but also great new opportunities.

Our success depends on how well we exploit our most valuable assets: our knowledge, skills, and creativity. These are the key to designing high-value goods and services and advanced business practices. They are at the heart of a modern, knowledge driven economy.

This new world challenges business to be innovative and creative, to improve performance continuously, to build new alliances and ventures. But it also challenges Government: to create and execute a new approach to industrial policy.

That is the purpose of this White Paper. Old-fashioned state intervention did not and cannot work. But neither does naive reliance on markets.

The Government must promote competition, stimulating enterprise, flexibility and innovation by opening markets. But we must also invest in British capabilities when companies alone cannot: in education, in science and in the creation of a culture of enterprise. And we must promote creative partnerships which help companies: to collaborate for competitive advantage; to promote a long term vision in a world of short term pressures; to benchmark their performance against the best in the world; and to forge alliances with other businesses and with employees. All this is the DTI's role.

We will not meet our objectives overnight. The White Paper creates a policy framework for the next ten years. We must compete more effectively in today's tough markets if we are to prosper in the markets of tomorrow.

In Government, in business, in our universities and throughout society we must do much more to foster a new entrepreneurial spirit: equipping ourselves for the long term, prepared to seize opportunities, committed to constant innovation and enhanced performance. That is the route to commercial success and prosperity for all. We must put the future on Britain's side.

Tony Blair

The Rt Hon Tony Blair MP, Prime Minister

Foreword sourced from Our Competitive Future: Building the Knowledge Driven Economy (Cm. 4167) Great Britain. Dept. of Trade & Industry (December 1998)

"The UK has more people who want to start a business than many other countries. Compared to the US, too few of these businesses achieve high growth. They lack a competitive edge and their founders often lack the ambition or capabilities to manage growth. The UK needs more risk takers."

Our Competitive Future: Building the Knowledge Driven Economy (Cm. 4167)

Great Britain. Dept. of Trade & Industry (December 1998)

If you were a small business entrepreneur, the Government needed you to *want* more. You had to embrace risk and reward, and to put it bluntly, grow a more "enhanced" set of business balls (metaphorically speaking of course). Only then would global competitiveness be realised in the UK.

Fighting Fear

It is easy to band about words such as ambition and risk when it is not your own money and life on the line. The implication that British businesses lacked guts seemed a tad unfair considering the UK was still the 5th largest world economy in 1998. However, the White Paper had raised a controversial but important hypothesis, that small and medium sized businesses did not sufficiently understand the concept of risk and reward to realise their potential. Marry that deficiency with an economy that vilified failure and the Government considered it serious enough to give out some fairly tough love. Tony Blair was characteristically blunt when he stated that we were all "too afraid of failure."[17]

One of the key objectives set out in the Knowledge Driven Economy was to de-stigmatise business failure in the United Kingdom. The White Paper observed that fear of failure was lower in the US, where entrepreneurs learnt from their mistakes, and were encouraged to try again. Contrast this with the UK business climate where investors are always cautious about your track record, where the stigma of bankruptcy is a life long sentence (socially if not legally), and the lessons of failure are viewed with contempt.

Too many start-ups were being discouraged by the perceived penalties of failure (social and financial). Worse still, those entrepreneurs that had shown guts and gained the hard earned lessons of business failure were now being needlessly lost to the economy – a knowledge hemorrhage of sorts.

Consider some of the higher profile business "failures", people who experienced the most painful, intensive training course that money can't buy – a business fatality.

- Henry Ford - his early businesses failed and left him broke five times before he founded the Ford Motor Company.
- Bill Gates - Started a failed first business with Microsoft co-founder Paul Allen called Traf-O-Data. Did okay in the end.
- Walt Disney – Prior to his cartoon dynasty Walt had 2 business failures with Iwers-Disney and Laugh-O-Grams (bankruptcy).
- Alan Sugar – Wound up his company Amstrad PLC in 1997. Re-launch business had sales of £96 million just nine years later.

Business failure is not a permanent state of being and success is not how many times you fall; it's how many times you get back up. But changing a country's culture would not be a quick fix. Practical barriers to returning to the entrepreneurial fold could be tackled head on and, as a statement of intent, the Government committed to changing laws on bankruptcy. Entrepreneurs would then be able to phoenix back more quickly from the ashes of business failure, much wiser for the experience.

In the Knowledge Driven Economy the new millennium mantra would be - if at first you don't succeed, try - try again.

Beefing Up the Benchmark

In 1998, enthusiasm for benchmarking had survived the change in government. In fact, the love affair appeared even more entrenched as the salvation for all our small business woes. The White Paper pledged a surge of funding to roll out a culture of benchmarking across the United Kingdom.

"Substantial" funding was committed to support the Confederation of British Industry's Fit for the Future campaign. This initiative was expected to yield a "massive increase" in best practice, targeting specifically the bulk of smaller organisations that "do not know where to start or how to build it into a business."

More significantly for the Business Link network and their customers, the Government outlined an expansion programme for the Benchmarking Index. The target for this programme was to ensure 50,000 businesses per annum (including 10,000 start ups) undertook "benchmarking or other best practice activity for the first time."

Knowledge Deposit

"Entrepreneurs often fail to realise the potential of their ideas because they lack the business skills they need. The key to competitive advantage in the knowledge driven economy is the capability of firms and other institutions to acquire and absorb knowledge, to exploit it to develop new products and processes."

Our Competitive Future

Building the Knowledge Driven Economy - December 1998.

If you were a small business, the Government had signalled intent to nurture your inner entrepreneur. Benchmarking would encourage you to look outside your business bubble and seek out best practice, but where was the bank of data needed to unleash this entrepreneurial feast?

Information without action is dead data. Knowledge, an unconscious understanding of the data, leads to a natural change in behaviour or belief. Or in layman's language, you learn to do something better instinctively. The Government would help improve entrepreneurial capability by creating a new bank of intelligence. Critical know-how needed for the future was deemed to be:

- Running the Knowledge Company

Small business owners needed the capability to create and constantly reinvent to become a "knowledge company." Effective knowledge management skills would be key to fostering an environment in business, where knowledge is recognised by all as a business asset, to be collected and codified (in a planned way). Continuous learning must be used every day to improve what you do.

The Government talked of a "whole literature on knowledge management." The DTI would grow this bank of information by producing new Access to Best Business Practice (ABBP) guides for businesses. These documents provided guidance on best practice, business tools and knowledge management. The Benchmark Index would contribute to this education, providing a formal framework to collect key performance data. But this alone would be insufficient to create a nation of knowledge savvy entrepreneurs.

An ever-present barrier to the Knowledge Company dream was the UK's traditional choice of company culture. Common in the majority of businesses in 1998 (and indeed today), command and control hierarchies do not exactly foster across the board knowledge sharing. It's hard to innovate if you use just one mind. In a war on apathy, government needed to win hearts and minds to change long held beliefs.

- Exploiting IT (+C)

1998 was a very different world. 33% of the general public couldn't see any benefit to using IT. 29% of businesses remained "indifferent or uncertain" about the issue. Just 8% of UK businesses had an IT Director (67% in the US).[18] The Internet explosion was igniting, with over one million new web pages being created, and 80,000 new users coming on-line every day during 1998.

To compete more effectively in the growing digital economy, businesses would require "new technologies, skills, people and mobile capital." IT and communications capability would underpin ability to innovate, to create and operate world-class processes, to exploit e-commerce and meet the ever growing needs of increasingly demanding customers. If you were a small business the Government *had* to open up your eyes to the importance of the digital economy, and fast.

The private sector was deemed to have inadequate resource and desire to address this issue within the required timescale. Out of this market failure was born the Information Society Initiative (ISI). Centres of Expertise would be opened across the Business Link network. These sites would provide access to expert data and the opportunity to speak to a specialist adviser, someone who could help plan how to exploit these findings for a profit. The ISI promised to set up 80 support centres across the UK providing impartial advice on how to exploit information and communication technologies (ICTs).

The Government promised this new programme would help one million small businesses prepare for the digital age. The plan was to achieve national coverage by the end of 1999. This commitment was backed up by a pledge to invest an additional £20 million of taxpayer funds over a three years period to support the project.

In the trading year for 1999 a total of 17,823 small and medium sized businesses in the UK accessed information and specialist advice at an ISI Centre.

Once again, the message was fairly unambiguous - modernize or die.

In 2000, the ISI would be re-branded UK Online for Business and the emphasis switched to the e-adoption ladder, moving business step by step from no IT infrastructure to advanced e-commerce. Just three years later the specialist advisers were swallowed into the revised Business Links.

ISI Centres were no more.

Heavy Hand Banned

"Governments must be sensitive to the changing needs of business in order to understand how policy can go with the grain of the market and be most effective. The approach must not be one of heavy-handed intervention."

The Rt Hon Peter Mandelson MP - Secretary of State for Trade and Industry

Our Competitive Future

Building the Knowledge Driven Economy - December 1998.

Business Links were now being challenged to "address deficiencies in entrepreneurial skill", as well as nuts and bolts business performance. Inspiration and enterprise were now key competences required in every Personal Business Adviser. Unfortunately, nothing in the 1998 toolkit was designed to build up this capability. Advisers had previously relied on their own experience and knowledge to draw out entrepreneurial thinking in small businesses. However, the new quantity driven agenda demanded a degree of standardisation to achieve the required efficiencies. Soft intangible aspects of business support, like the ability to inspire, were akin to alchemy and were viewed with suspicion. The philosophy appeared to be, if you can't measure it, you can't manage it, dismiss it.

The drive for a national programme of entrepreneurial stimulus was inherently flawed from the start. Quality would always be dependent on each Personal Business Adviser's unique personality and personal background.

Micro measurement is not a comfortable bedfellow for creativity and innovation, let alone inspiration, but the die was cast in the Knowledge Driven White Paper. The Government would instigate a decade long policy of blanket benchmarking *their* own performance in a bid to raise standards across the country. This approach would reach to the tips of the furthest tentacles in the Business Link network.

Personal Business Advisers could no longer retain a simple "seek out and help" brief. The Knowledge Driven agenda demanded this expensive resource deliver a specific suite of support, targeted at achieving measurable outputs. Lord Mandelson had spoken.
"Heavy handed" intervention was out.

Small businesses would no longer have a subsidised business consultant (as some would have you believe) to meet their needs. The new Personal Business Adviser service was taking a first tentative step towards "light touch" and peddling the top down small business agenda of the Government. Mother knows best if you will.

The inherent conflict of interest in Business Link, customer or paymaster first, was a constant source of friction within Business Links over the next 13 years, albeit most initiatives would have at least some value to the small business. The Business Link was changing. If you ran a small business, *you* had to change too.

CHAPTER FIVE

QUALITY MARKS

1999

"We still have a considerable duplication of effort at a local level. From a business point of view, it's a muddle, from a funding point of view - it's a waste of resource. The way forward is a single unified business organisation at a local level. It presumes that the existing approved Chamber network, Training and Enterprise Councils and Business Links will disappear."

Mr Ian Peters

British Chambers of Commerce Director-General

The Future Chamber: Integrated Local Business Support for 2000 and Beyond (1997)

The Labour Government was certainly not alone in thinking the Business Links must change. Even at this early stage there were calls from the business support sector to halt the project.

Speaking for YOU

In the United Kingdom there are three mainstream groups representing businesses – the British Chambers of Commerce, the Federation of Small Businesses and the Confederation of British Industry. These organisations have the Government's ear on all issues relating to business. Their power base for lobbying is founded on a mix of membership and history. These organisations presume to speak for all business people, whether members or not, whether they like it or not. The British Chambers of Commerce is fairly clear about this, categorically stating that they "serve not only its member businesses but the wider business community."[19]

Majority Interests

In 2010, the Department for Business, Innovation and Skills announced there were 4.5 million businesses trading in the United Kingdom. 64.2% of these organisations were sole proprietorships with no employees, presumably single person operations.

The Federation of Small Businesses (FSB) claim to be the "UK's largest campaigning pressure group." In 2011, this organisation held a membership of 200,000 businesses, across 33 regions and 194 branches.[20] Statistically, their voice speaks for 4.5 percent of entrepreneurs (business population) in the United Kingdom.

The Confederation of British Industry (CBI) represents 200,000 businesses, of which 2,000 are direct members. The rest are affiliate members through 180 trade organisations. Even using this by association calculation, that is still just a 4.4 percent representation.

The British Chambers of Commerce (BCC) is "the national body for a powerful and influential Network of Accredited Chambers of Commerce across the UK." Their 2010 National Benchmarking Survey confirmed an increase in the "the total number of businesses represented by the Accredited Network to 92,120", representing a market share of 2.0 percent of entrepreneurs in the country. [21]

These three organisations hold some great business minds and undoubtedly add value for their fee-paying members. But speaking for the majority? You decide.

To set this in context, in 2010, Mark Prisk MP, Minister of State for Business and Enterprise, confirmed over 750,000 organisations in England had accessed Business Link for help in the previous twelve months.[22] That total was 19.7 percent market penetration, and more than the direct membership of Chambers, FSB and CBI combined.

Chamber Plot

In 1997, the British Chambers of Commerce acknowledged an "improvement in the quality of local business support" since the formation of Business Link. "Business Links were a major step in the right direction in the rationalisation of business services." However, their Green Paper, The Future Chamber, stated categorically the network was "confusing, wasteful of resource and lacks sustainability."[23] Their vision was one without a Business Link, "absorbing" the service into a merger of Training and Enterprise Councils, and the respective regional Chambers in each area. Consolidation of the different interests would create a super agency, with the British Chambers of Commerce influence assured. To be fair this idea was not a new one, Lord Heseltine had mooted such a formal merger at the outset but received a lukewarm response, "I spent a lot of time trying to persuade the TECs and Chambers to merge."[24] However, the British Chambers of Commerce resisted this blanket merger, reluctant to sell out the autonomy and independence of their affiliates. Each Chamber in the network would be free to decide their destiny. Even so, ten Chambers had already merged with TECs by 1998. In 1997 the British Chambers of Commerce had revised their policy, but on the basis that it is always better to lead than follow.

In 2011, the founder of Business Link was far less charitable when recalling the British Chambers of Commerce position.

"They themselves should have set up this combined advisory service. They should have gone to Government and said, look you've got all these services, work with us and create the one stop shop. That's what they should have done. We did it for them."

The Rt Hon the Lord Heseltine CH

Interview with author at Haymarket Head Office, Hammersmith - 8th June, 2011

The Octopus and Tentacles

Enterprise Agencies are the fourth most influential business support group in England, after the Chambers, FSB and CBI. In 2011, over 250,000 businesses accessed business support via Enterprise Agencies. The National Federation of Enterprise Agencies stated that their independent member organisations aimed to be the "preferred route to market for those wishing to engage with our market (small and medium sized businesses)."

Enterprise Agencies were already delivering business support prior to the advent of Business Links in 1993. As a result, these businesses always had most to lose in the event of a successful Business Link, and whilst working relationships were developed in the interests of the customer, more often than not they were spiked by rivalry. On 2nd June, 1998, in the Select Committee for Trade and Industry, Mr Lindsay Hoyle, (Labour MP for Chorley) accused Business Links of "trying to kill off Enterprise Agencies." The rationale for this accusation was a perceived duplication of service and competition for existing services.

"What has happened is instead of working together the Business Link has been like an octopus, tentacles have been spreading everywhere to try and take over everybody else's role and there has been duplication all the way through. You talked about marriage and I think the way they have been going is creating divorces all through the different agencies."

Mr Lindsay Hoyle MP

Select Committee for Trade and Industry Minutes - 2 June 1998

Mr Hoyle believed small businesses were already getting exactly what was needed and that Business Link was an unnecessary intervention. Far from challenging this view, Barbara Roche MP (Enhanced Business Links) actually reinforced the stereotype by blaming the Conservative set up of Business Link and claiming "because Business Link was the flavour of the month the Enterprise Agencies just got ignored."[25] On the ground, getting off on the wrong foot would always make true partnership working a challenge. This situation was further complicated by the Enterprise Agencies being frequent sub-contractors for Business Links. Business Link Partnerships received the bulk of government funding and would commonly contract out start up support to their 'partner'. It is difficult to maintain a partnership of equals, when one of the parties has the other in their pocket.

Small businesses could benefit greatly from working with both organisations, accessing specialist micro / start up support at the Enterprise Agencies before moving to Business Link for next phase advice. Yet cross referral of clients between Business Link and the Agencies was less than prolific, even though this should have been a symbiotic relationship in the best interest of small business.

"We need to implement this agenda for action as quickly as possible if we are to enhance the Business Link service so that it continues to meet your requirements as its customers. The Government is only one of the partners involved in delivering this agenda. The British Chambers of Commerce, the Local Government Association, the TEC National Council and the National Federation of Enterprise Agencies have, together with their local constituents, a crucial role in developing a Business Link service."

Barbara Roche MP, Under Secretary of State for Small Firms, Trade & Industry

Enhanced Business Links – A Vision for the 21st Century

Great Britain Department of Trade and Industry October 1997

The supporters of business were talking; and government was listening.

Rationalisation

On 28th October, 1999, Patricia Hewitt, Minister of State for Small Business and E-Commerce, announced that the existing 81 Business Link contracts would be discontinued, and new bids were invited to become one of 45 new Business Link franchisees. Once again the winners of these bids would be given instruction, but retain local discretion on how best to serve their region's business needs. The structure of the bidding organisations would not be dictated.

"I start from the basis that the profile of individual businesses is different around the country, therefore the way in which business support is conducted may be a bit different and what I do not want to do is to force, if you like, the business support partners into a uniform pattern throughout the country."

Barbara Roche, MP Parliamentary Under-Secretary of State for Small Firms, Trade & Industry. House of Commons Select Committee of Trade and Industry – 2nd June 1998

The partners in each area would be free to decide how best to work together, some preferring formal mergers, others informal collaborative working. The Government's main priority was to see public money safeguarded. As a result, using this evolutionary approach, whatever the structure, all bidding organisations would be put under the microscope to ensure they passed due diligence.

On 2nd June, 1998, Jim Reid, Director of Business Link, told the Select Committee there were some areas already where "you have got the TEC and the Chamber and Business Link working very happily together but they want to retain their independence. That is absolutely fine if they are delivering the service to their local business and I think it is actually important that we do allow that local flexibility." [26] However, when new mergers were proposed the over riding litmus test would be whether an overall "improvement in the service to the customer" would be achieved. If so, "we tend to smile on it", said Jim Reid. If the merger did not satisfy this requirement then the Government would be "at least more agnostic."

"What I did not want to happen was for every Business Link to reinvent the wheel, to offer exactly the same identical service because it was not meshing in with the reality of the local business profile."

Barbara Roche, MP Parliamentary Under-Secretary of State for Small Firms, Trade &
Industry. House of Commons Select Committee of Trade and Industry – 2nd June 1998

Business Link would have 45% fewer Operators, but no less variability. Future differences between the regions would not be accidental; they were by design.

Quality Marks

In the Enhanced Business Links vision, Margaret Beckett (the newly appointed President of the Board of Trade) had been crystal clear about her priorities for Business Links – "quality, quality, and quality." These concerns preceded the findings of the first full and independent review of Business Link performance.

In October 1998, the Public and Corporate Economic Consultants (PACEC) published "Business Links - Value for Money Evaluation." This DTI commissioned report concluded that small and medium sized businesses did indeed grow if they used Business Link. Over a three years period, an "average" customer increased sales by £55,000 and employed 1.63 more personnel. These were the "attributed" gains from Business Link. In real terms, organisations were found to have increased sales by £76,000, profits by £9,000, exports by £6,000 and net assets by £13,000. "From the qualitative analysis the results indicated that business growth can be attributed directly to Business Links."[27]

The report also concluded that, during the period 1994 to 1997, the Business Link network helped create 8,000 jobs, nearly £1 billion of extra sales, £145 million of net assets, £400 million of export revenue and over £300 million additional profit. However, the same research found customer perception to be far less clear. One in five of intensively assisted businesses (those with a Personal Business Adviser) believed their gains would have been achieved without Business Link i.e. "total deadweight." One in four believed the gains would have been realised without Business Link but their help did "accelerate" the progress. This apparent disconnect between the quantitative findings of research and the subjective views of small businesses would help others build a case against Business Link in the future. It is worth noting that 40 percent of entrepreneurs still stated categorically they would *not* have achieved the gains without Business Link.

The Secretary of State for Trade and Industry, Patricia Hewitt, did not mention any of the 1998 findings when she later asserted that Business Link was "in a pretty pathetic state when we took over." It didn't really matter. In 1998, it was the dawning of the continuous improvement agenda and "stretching" targets for everyone, not a time for pats on the back. Besides, the taxpaying entrepreneur would always deserve more. Just on principle, value for money on public coffers is never enough.

Regional autonomy was one thing, but the Business Link rationalisation would not come without a set of imposed conditions and controls from Central Government. Or put in government speak – "Action to strengthen our quality assurance arrangements so that, as customers, you have confidence in the Business Link brand as a hallmark of quality and as taxpayers, confidence that our expenditure on these services represents value for money."[28]

Test 1 - Trouble at the Top

"I firmly believe that all Business Link partnerships must develop a real entrepreneurial and commercial culture if they are to be credible in the eyes of their customers. I am therefore working with the Institute of Directors to develop a framework for Board development which we can introduce for all Business Link partnerships to use as quickly as possible."

Barbara Roche MP, Under Secretary of State for Small Firms, Trade & Industry

Enhanced Business Links – A Vision for the 21st Century

Great Britain Department of Trade and Industry October 1997

The first condition for Business Link accreditation was directly targeted at the people running each new franchise. The Accreditation Advisory Board demanded evidence that the people at the helm of each Business Link had the required "background", "experience" and "leadership" credentials. Only then would the Business Link brand have "credibility with the local business community."

Furthermore the Department of Trade and Industry (DTI) insisted that each individual Business Link board demonstrate a private sector presence from small and medium sized businesses. These Directors were not to be sourced from the usual suspects i.e. Chambers, TECs and Business Link themselves. These independents would "act as the voice of the customer" and ensure any direction taken was in the best interests of the businesses using the service, not the agencies. This condition assumed existing Business Link boards were deficient in these areas, otherwise why the need for change?

This first test was seen as pivotal to "making Business Links more Business-Like." From 1998, the Accreditation Advisory Board would only recommend accreditation of Business Links that "clearly demonstrate that they have developed the required entrepreneurial culture."

Test 2 – Pay Your Way

"A key test of whether a Business Link partnership is providing the services customers want, is whether those customers are prepared to pay for the service. I do not believe that an organisation, which continues to rely entirely on public funding, can ever become the customer driven organisation, which you want. That is why the Government will continue to set targets for Business Link partnerships in terms of the proportion of their income which is raised by charges to their customers."

Barbara Roche MP, Under Secretary of State for Small Firms, Trade & Industry

Enhanced Business Links – A Vision for the 21st Century

Great Britain Department of Trade and Industry October 1997

The second new condition appeared primarily driven by a demand for self-sufficiency, albeit this was pitched as a necessary step on the path to a more entrepreneurial culture.

The DTI argued that like any other business, Business Links must deliver a service that customers will value and want to use again and again. This value would only be proven if the small and medium sized businesses were willing to put their hand in their pocket to pay for the service. Business Links were encouraged to "bring in private sector services wherever possible" to meet this goal. This was not an optional requirement. The DTI set out a written condition that by "their fifth year of operations, Business Link partnerships must earn 25% of the income needed for their Business Link branded services from the businesses they assist."[29] The majority of Business Link partnerships would struggle to meet this challenge.

In 1998, the Business Link philosophy inherent in most partnerships was 'free at the point of delivery'. After all, the taxpaying entrepreneur had already indirectly paid for the service. The Business Link brand had been active in the market for almost 5 years. Tens of thousands of customers had personal experience of getting something for nothing and were quite bemused by the fact that should now have to start paying. We are trying to "develop an entrepreneurial culture" wasn't much consolation.

Worse still, the pay to play caveat did nothing to ease the suspicions of consultants in the private sector. Barbara Roche MP was insistent that "developing an entrepreneurial culture and an effective charging policy does not mean unfair competition. A condition of DTI funding is that Business Links must not compete unfairly with the unsubsidised private sector." Not very reassuring when the new Business Links were being told a condition of survival was hitting a 25% income target. People tend to do what they need to do when their future is on the line.

Finally, Barbara Roche spelt out that the "business of a Business Link is to provide services - at a price small and medium sized enterprises can afford - that otherwise would not be available to them, not to duplicate services already available in the market place." Time to think of some valuable new products, services no one in the private sector had already thought of, and charge the customers not much. That should work.

Undoubtedly, some Business Link partnerships were more commercially minded than others, and the goal of becoming more enterprising is valid. It is also justifiable to try and end dependence on public funding, if at all possible. The commerciality clause would drive each Business Link to offer variable flavours of the service in different regions, some chargeable, some not. Not based only on the needs of their local entrepreneurs, but on an urgent need to pay the Government's own way. A postcode lottery determined whether you needed your wallet.

Test 3 – Improvement Movement

"I want to ensure that all Business Link partnerships develop a culture, which is dedicated to continuous improvement in the service they provide and develop the mechanisms required to support and sustain it."

Barbara Roche MP, Under Secretary of State for Small Firms, Trade & Industry

Enhanced Business Links – A Vision for the 21st Century

Great Britain Department of Trade and Industry October 1997

From April 1998, accredited Business Links would be required to monitor and report on the impact of their performance. If you were a small business customer, these impact measures would be determined by how well *you* were doing in business. If you were not improving productivity, profitability and export, Business Link would be judged to be failing. In the new Tony Blair era of openness, any failings would not be discrete. The DTI committed to publishing "league tables of comparative performance" for Business Links for all to see, motivation with a large dose of healthy competition / humiliation. On the issue of Business Link improvement, the Government would not leave this to chance, making use of the Business Excellence Model mandatory. This quality model demands organisations focus in on nine elements, a mix of "enablers" (how we do things) and "results" (what we target, measure and achieve). The DTI would now have access to "a comprehensive, systematic and regular review" of

Business Links. Their progress would be benchmarked not only within their own peer group, but compared to thousands of the best businesses in Europe.

"Business Links for the first time across the country have got to collect measures which actually do look at their effectiveness countrywide, so they do give us a measure." "If it looks as if a particular Business Link is not delivering then clearly that Business Link will not be sustainable."

Barbara Roche, MP Parliamentary Under-Secretary of State for Small Firms, Trade & Industry. House of Commons Select Committee of Trade and Industry – 2nd June 1998

This decision did introduce a degree of accountability to the network, but crunching numbers would press ever-increasing administration demands on the Business Link partnerships. In 2010, an internal survey of a Personal Business Adviser team in Business Link found that client related work constituted just 29.4% of adviser time.[30] Monitoring and reporting performance is a vital ingredient for any organisation, but when two thirds of the most expensive resource is spent not serving the end customer, it might be time to stop counting and start asking some difficult questions.

Test 4 - Satisfaction Guaranteed

"While each Business Link is an independent organisation, all Business Links are part of a national network in which we have all invested in order to secure high nationally agreed standards. I intend to strengthen further the existing accreditation arrangements and will not hesitate to withdraw government funding and the use of the brand from Business Link partnerships which fail to meet or sustain the required standards."

Barbara Roche MP, Under Secretary of State for Small Firms, Trade & Industry
Enhanced Business Links – A Vision for the 21st Century
Great Britain Department of Trade and Industry October 1997

The new Business Link franchisees would be under constant scrutiny to ensure their service met "high minimum standards which are constantly raised across the Business Link network."

The Government did not own the Business Link partnerships and quality remained the responsibility of each individual Board. Therefore, influence rather than command would be used to engineer the required improvements. The Government wanted a radical change in quality across the network, not in patches. A "rigorously enforced" audit of the national contract would be their change agent.[31]

The Labour Government was adamant that "no Business Link could be accredited without a recent certificate of audit." This condition was not lip service.

"The current accreditation criteria are not easy to meet. So far only 14 Business Links have become fully accredited. Every one of them has said that it has found the process extremely tough. What is more, a number of Business Links have had to engage in further development work following their first application for accreditation before they have been finally accredited."

Barbara Roche MP, Under Secretary of State for Small Firms, Trade & Industry

Enhanced Business Links – A Vision for the 21st Century

Great Britain Department of Trade and Industry October 1997

The Government had made a steadfast commitment to "monitor, systematically and carefully", whether the "taxpayers' investment is being repaid."

"When we talk about small businesses, there is a temptation there of talking about small businesses as if they are all the same; they are not of course. They are different according to the different size within that definition. They are different according to the sector they operate in. They are different in that a third generation family-run business is very different perhaps from a high-tech start-up. There is a range there."

Barbara Roche MP, Under Secretary of State for Small Firms, Trade & Industry

Enhanced Business Links – A Vision for the 21st Century

Great Britain Department of Trade and Industry October 1997

When the DTI first launched Business Link, rather than spread the jam too thin, the partnerships in the network had been instructed to target their finite resources at businesses employing between 10 to 249 employees.

The new Business Link franchisees would not be so fortunate.

"Many of you - including the Federation of Small Businesses and the Forum of Private Business - told me that you believed the Business Link service was only for larger businesses and that Business Links were not interested in any business with fewer than 10 employees. I can promise you that any business, regardless of size, will be able to find services to meet its needs at its Business Link... there should be something for everyone."

Barbara Roche MP, Under Secretary of State for Small Firms, Trade & Industry

Enhanced Business Links – A Vision for the 21st Century

Great Britain Department of Trade and Industry October 1997

The caveat that Business Links should be "providing a Service for All Small and Medium Sized Businesses", effectively opened the door to over 3 million customers. The policy may have been fair, ensuring all the taxpayers could claim a return on their investment. However, with less than a thousand Personal Business Advisers employed in the entire country, Business Links would have to be enterprising in the extreme to meet the Government's ever-increasing demand for market "penetration." In 1999, a Personal Business Adviser would typically be tasked to support 30 growth businesses per annum. In 2008, this target was nearer 100 customers. Simple mathematics said an adviser had 66% less time to help each business in their portfolio.

Test 5 – People Quality

The final factor influencing accreditation of a Business Link would be "people quality." The Government would "make sure that Business Links employ top quality people" to create the standards small businesses "were entitled to expect."[32]

The business support sector had never had a universally recognised industry standard for advisory excellence. The closest credible comparisons were academic qualifications such as Master of Business Administration (MBA) and association standards such as Chartered Institute of Marketing (CIM).

In the nineties, Personal Business Advisers were recruited based on their experience, particularly evidence of running their own business. However, the subjective nature of this selection process created a strain of variability throughout the Business Link network. This inconsistency was no longer acceptable. In the future Business Links would have to report ongoing evidence that *all* personnel were up to the job.

Strategic Shift

The Business Link Tracker Study in 2001 appeared to confirm all had not been well with the network in recent years. This report concluded that from 1996 to 2000 there was "little evidence that Business Link was targeted effectively at firms with a track record of rapid prior growth." In addition, the authors concluded the same was true about value of the assistance itself, showing no "significant effect on firms' sales, employment or productivity growth performance."

Even more seriously, in the Tracker report only 25% of small and medium sized businesses reported any additionality from using Business Link services.

This study contradicted earlier studies. The PACEC report just three years earlier, which covered 1994 to 1996, concluded that "working with Business Link over a three years period increased your sales by £55,000, helped you employ 1.63 more personnel" and was magnanimous in it's praise of attributable impact.[33]

Without pre-judging either survey, as the famous quote goes, "I abhor averages. I like the individual case. A man may have six meals one day and none the next, making an average of three meals per day, but that is not a good way to live."[34]

All together now

The Government was not alone in seeking quality improvements and consistency.

"I think what Barbara Roche is seeking to do is bring standards up. We're as good as the weakest point in our chain. It's important that every single Business Link represents the brand. In a way it's like a franchise - you need consistent quality."

Ms Valerie Thompson, Chief Executive, Business Link London Central

UK Business Link Proves its Worth By Robert Gray

Published in Management Today magazine. 1st October 1997

The newly strengthened Business Link Network Company (BLNC) would echo this sentiment. The BLNC had been formed to represent all the Business Link operators around the country. The Government believed a strong BLNC was important to drive out any inconsistency in the network. So much so, that in 1998, the Government backed the organisation with a pump-priming grant to appoint a full time Chief Executive for the first time (Peter Sinclair) and quadruple staff from two to eight.

The Government exerted further pressure more directly by appointing a team of full-time regional managers to "make sure good practice is exchanged between the different areas and monitor the delivery of the standards under the contract." [35]

Barbara Roche MP remained encouraged by the attitude of the Business Links.

"What is particularly encouraging is that when I introduced the vision statement it has been, as I say, very warmly embraced not only by the personal business advisors who are the main people who deliver the service from the Links, but also by the Chairmen and Chief Executives as well. They really do want to pull up the service as much as they possibly can."

Barbara Roche, MP Parliamentary Under-Secretary of State for Small Firms, Trade & Industry. House of Commons Select Committee of Trade and Industry – 2nd June 1998

It was early days. The Government was effectively using a performance management approach to engineer the changes it believed were needed in Business Links. Whilst a proven, if rather soulless, method to hit targets, performance management only works if you have access to timely and accurate management data. Knowing exactly how you are doing at the right time is a critical commodity in this model.

As a result Business Links would have to re-deploy an increased share of their resource to deal with the added administration / IT burden, the only way to ensure the DTI's audit and contractual demands would be met. A budget that had previously been invested in frontline support for small and medium sized businesses.

CHAPTER SIX

BANKERS, WHIZ KIDS AND FAILED BUSINESS PEOPLE

"I visited many Business Link centres, which I understand are funded in some way by government although I am not at all clear how. To be perfectly frank, apart from meeting a nice bunch of people, there was no real business advice dished out other than simple stuff you could pick up and learn for yourself by going on the Internet."

Lord Alan Sugar
House of Lords Debate, Hansard – 24th March, 2011

In 1999, the Government set out their intentions clearly in writing. Business Links must address "people quality" issues or their mandate would be withdrawn.

It is not an uncommon view in this country, that if you have not actually started a business yourself and made a million, you have nothing useful to say. This belief was at the heart of most attacks on the quality of Business Link people. If you were so damn good, why on earth were you working at Business Link and not doing it yourself - a fair question.

"When Patricia Hewitt was Minister for Small Business she made it one of the key criteria in the bidding guidance for the new Small Business Service contracts back in 2000 that advisers should have experience of being an entrepreneur...We are very, very clear that we want our front-line advisers to have had experience in starting and growing their own businesses. We want the services and businesses on the ground to be run by entrepreneurs for entrepreneurs."

Mr Martin Wyn Griffith, Chief Executive of the Small Business Service

House of Commons Trade and Industry Minutes of Evidence 6th Jan, 2004

If the Personal Business Advisers offered so much, why would they choose to opt for service in a government-funded agency? To many this question was inexplicable and the only logical conclusion must be these people couldn't cut it in the private sector (it is worth noting at this point that Business Link Operators were, of course, private sector organisations themselves).

Life Work Balance

Anyone who has run a business, successful or otherwise, will know that it is the most demanding challenge to take on. Long working hours, uncertainty in the extreme (particularly financial) and infringements into your personal life are par for the course (it is very difficult to leave your problems at work). These costs are the price of independence and unlimited earning potential. Conversely, anyone who has failed in business incurs emotional and financial scars. The very best entrepreneurs fast track dealing with these issues and get right back to business. However, the majority must work out these complex issues in their own time, some take longer than others.

Whether negative or positive drivers, choosing a life work balance is not a weakness, whatever personalities in the media may have you believe. This act does not make knowledge any less valuable to a small business. In fact, the knowledge probably becomes more valuable, as the individual acutely feels both the joy and pain of business. *Empathy* is *the* key competence needed in any business adviser.

Even if successful, the Institute of Directors acknowledges "down shifting" as a modern phenomenon, where successful people choose to forgo high ambition for quality of life.[36] In 2000, the man responsible for Business Links himself was one such person.

"May I be personal and say people like me who have started and grown their own businesses in the creative industries, who decided after 10 years that there was more to life than doing what I was doing and wanted to get out and find another vehicle for my career, went to Henley to do an MBA and fell in love with strategic planning, was way too old to be employed by the big four consultancies and discovered in 1996 a thing that Michael Heseltine had set up called Business Link."

Mr Martin Wyn Griffith, Chief Executive of the Small Business Service
House of Commons – Public Accounts Minutes of Evidence 19th June, 2006

That's not to say the Personal Business Adviser team was infallible.

"There are several thousand advisers out there and this is a human system. Not everybody is perfect in the world. Occasionally we get a mishap."

Mr Martin Wyn Griffith, Chief Executive of the Small Business Service
House of Commons Trade and Industry Minutes of Evidence 6th January, 2004

The Mishap Cap

"The quality of any service depends ultimately on the quality of its people. We will discuss with the appropriate professional bodies the introduction of a comprehensive range of national standards of professional competence for all those delivering Business Link branded services, with the aim of introducing them within 6 months. I also propose to review in 12 months time whether we should make such standards mandatory."

Ms Barbara Roche MP, Parliamentary Under Secretary of State for Small Firms
Enhanced Business Links - A Vision for the 21st Century - Oct 8th 1997

In 1997, despite prior independent research suggesting the Personal Business Adviser service was fit for purpose, the Labour Government embarked on a determined campaign to engineer some expertise and consistency into the team. Organic recruitment policies just weren't enough anymore. The Government was determined to guarantee a level of quality that small businesses had a right to expect. Whilst the Department of Trade and Industry had previously gone out of their way not to be prescriptive, ensuring Business Links had freedom to innovate, on this issue there was no room for manoeuvre. The wheels of a national accreditation scheme for advisers were in motion.

Competency Breeds Contempt

"I am not thinking of paper and pen exercises. I am thinking of very practical professional qualifications that we would expect the Personal Business Advisers to have. The vast majority of our PBAs have either worked in a small business or have run or managed their business which is useful, because if they are going to give advice they have really got to come from a background where they have been there and done it and also suffered all the anxieties that a small business manager has."

Ms Barbara Roche MP, Parliamentary Under Secretary of State for Small Firms
House of Commons Trade and Industry Minutes of Evidence 2nd June 1998

In 2000, the Government (DTI) appointed Small Firms Enterprise Development Initiative Ltd (SFEDI) as the UK Standards Setting Body for Business Support and Business Enterprise. This organisation was tasked with managing and developing National Standards of Professional Competence. The Small Firm Enterprise Development Initiative (SFEDI) standard was born.

Barbara Roche MP claimed the specification for the standards had been developed with groups and associations such as the Institute of Business Advisers. However, the output from this process appeared firmly centred on satisfying a minimum performance level rather than stimulating excellence.

In 1997, the Enhanced Business Links paper had stressed that Business Link advisers must demonstrate sufficient knowledge in all aspects of business, from export right through to financial appraisal. These levels of knowledge would be maintained using continuous assessment against agreed Standards. The effectiveness of this strategy may have been slightly undermined by the setting of the grade itself.

The resulting standard was one-dimensional. If advisers satisfied the SFEDI grade they received the same "met" grading. Everyone received the same certificate and badge to show they were competent to practice business advice. It is difficult to see how this approach could do anything except encourage a culture of competence, rather than driving up expertise in the adviser team.

Consequently, the standards never had a high degree of credibility to advisers in the field, and probably even less in the wider business population, who in the main had never heard of the qualification. For example, whilst Business Link Norfolk invested heavily in the assessment process and contracted three national consultants to test the advisers against the standard, only one adviser out of thirty failed to satisfy the criteria at the first attempt. Even then that person was told it was impossible to "fail", to study up on their identified weaknesses and sit again.

Was this an impressive accolade for the Business Link or a damning judgement on the levels of knowledge demanded by the standard? Most likely, it was a little of both. A lack of challenge for the vast majority of business advisers working in Business Links would always be an issue for SFEDI credibility. On the plus side, in the absence of any standard at all, something was probably better than nothing!

A License to Practice

"We are going to be for the first time assessing all the advisers against those new standards and creating a corporate university, if you like, a business school for business support, in an effort to achieve a quantum leap in the quality of service which is being delivered."

David Irwin – Chief Executive of the Small Business Service
Select Committee on Trade and Industry - Wednesday 2nd May, 2001.

SFEDI standards would be mandatory for Business Link advisers. Advisers were barred from helping small businesses if they had not yet satisfied the assessment. Introducing a national standard was intended to guarantee a minimum level of service. If the adviser didn't make the grade, they were deemed unfit to help small and medium sized businesses.

The Government did not issue a similar mandatory instruction on how to complete the SFEDI assessment. Each Business Link had the freedom to select how best to prepare their staff for the test and who their assessors would be. This approach was a bit like asking turkeys to vote for Christmas. It was clearly in each Business Link's interest to ensure their employees satisfied the standard as quickly as possible, minimising cost and ensuring advisers were working in the field. As a result the assessment process varied greatly from region to region and it was difficult to compare like for like. To some it could appear a lot of money and time had been invested to rubber stamp the existing staff.

Regardless of the actual value added for small businesses, at the very least government could now claim a fully accredited workforce when challenged by critics.

The Second Coming of SFEDI

"One is creating a set of national standards of professional competence against which all new advisers in the first year must be assessed and they must form learning and development plans against those standards of professional competence."

Mr Martin Wyn Griffith, Chief Executive of the Small Business Service
House of Commons Trade and Industry Minutes of Evidence 6th January, 2004

Despite the proviso that accreditation was time bound and would lapse after a two year period, by the time the renewal dates arrived the mandatory status seemed to have slipped significantly down the agenda. Existing staff already had a certificate and reappraisal costs may have appeared prohibitive, even unnecessary, as customer satisfaction had risen constantly since the year 2000, showing no signs of decline. No research had been identified directly linking this improvement to the introduction of National Standards, but then none had been found saying it didn't help either. As a result the importance of SFEDI gradually slipped down the agenda, albeit the standards were still supported by the Department of Trade and Industry. Following the initial national adoption of SFEDI standards a comprehensive assessment of the network would not take place again for six years. The National Standards of Professional Competence had become a one off event, rather than a catalyst for continuous improvement in the Personal Business Adviser team.

In 2007, the second coming of SFEDI arrived. This renaissance was driven by the Regional Development Agencies who had assumed day-to-day responsibility for Business Links. One step removed from day to day operations, these organisations had been concerned with people quality from the start. The Regional Development Agencies demanded up to date accreditation of the advisers using a beefed up SFEDI standard. Once again, it would be mandatory in Business Links for all customer-facing advisers to be certified prior to helping businesses in the field. Lessons had been learnt and regional contracts were awarded to assessors who were independent of the Business Links. The process had more structure and a second grading level was introduced. Now an adviser could reach a standard or "gold" status, albeit distinguishing between the two was not easy. Disappointingly, the scheme still seemed fundamentally based on measuring competence, rather than stimulating excellence.

The Regional Development Agency had their assurance that Business Link was using competent people to deliver advice. However, each Business Link operator had committed a significant amount of adviser time and money to meeting this contractual demand, resource that could have been used to help small businesses.

The robustness of any quality standard must be measured in equal measure by how many candidates do and don't make the grade. If everyone passes fairly easily, what is the point of the assessment? In a decade working and meeting Business Link advisers, I have met only one adviser who failed to make the SFEDI grade at first attempt. A case of if it wasn't broken perhaps.

Electric BLU

Not content with National Standards, the Government went a step further by financing a Business Link University.

"The Business Link 'University' (BLU) has been established for the Small Business Service (SBS), Business Link Operators (BLO) and partners, fulfilling the 2001 Small Business Manifesto commitment to 'Create a Business University for Business Support'. The 'U' is the world's first virtual corporate university for business development professionals."

Patricia Hewitt, Minister for Small Business and E-Commerce
House of Commons Written Answers to Questions 22nd July, 2002

The rationale behind the creation of the BLU was sound. Due to the remote nature of the role, it was fairly rare for Business Advisers to share knowledge amongst themselves, let alone across a national network of independent organisations.

The Business Link University would be a web-based portal enabling advisers to swap ideas, network online and to complete training modules as required. It was not just for advisers, but also for Chief Executives and all levels of staff.

The structure of the online University was built on proven blue chip principles.

"We have a continuous development programme supported by a corporate university modelled on the Unipart Corporate University. This will enable organisations to share good practice, to learn from each other and learn from the best outside the organisation as well and get some economies of scale into training and development."

Mr Martin Wyn Griffith, Chief Executive of the Small Business Service
House of Commons - Trade and Industry Minutes of Evidence 6th January, 2004

How could this help an adviser give better advice in the field?

The set up cost of the Business Link University had been £1.42 million of taxpayer funds, so some sort of performance improvement was definitely expected. Each member of personnel was required to register on the website, but it would never be mandatory to undertake the training. This softly-softly strategy was based on an assumption that the BLU would become "synonymous with high quality learning" and this alone would make it the preferred choice for advisers across the network.

In 2002, electronic learning was a fairly new concept in the United Kingdom. Like any Internet community, usage was sporadic. Some users embraced the technology and some steered well clear. At the risk of being ageist, at the end of the nineties the average age of advisers was between 30 and 50, most being nearer the top end of the scale than the low end. Web skills were not instinctive as they are today.

The Business Link University did some valuable and costly analysis (which no doubt sits on a strong shelf somewhere), but to your typical business adviser it was not an essential requirement for their main reason to be, helping customers. Consequently, take up was never comprehensive. The relatively small percentage of advisers active on the forum accessed a much smaller pond of best practice than had originally been hoped for.

The Business Link University had the potential to transform levels of knowledge in the Personal Business Adviser team. However, ultimately the initiative was never widely embraced by advisers working with small and medium sized businesses.

Despite investing millions of taxpayer funds, that alone wouldn't be enough to stop the project, particularly as the need for consistency was still high on the agenda.

"We have squeezed the gap in satisfaction levels between each of the 45 operators. We have halved that gap, so it is a much more consistent network. Recognition of that point, and I take it at face value, is also one of the reasons why we have invested regularly in what we call "The BLU", our corporate university. We have been spending £1 million a year making sure that the entire network of advisers, chief executives, advice team managers has the ability to share knowledge."

Mr Martin Wyn Griffith, Chief Executive of the Small Business Service
House of Commons – Public Accounts Minutes of Evidence 19th June, 2006

Whether ahead of it's time or trying to force a team of square pegs into round holes, when it came to quality of advisers the Business Link University did little to persuade the doubters.

Myth Busting

In the nineties, contrary to popular belief, independent research suggests business advisers were actually highly qualified and experienced. A 1997 census of Personal Business Advisers found they were unlikely to be "whiz kids" fresh out of college, with 98 percent of the team over the age of 30 years old. This same survey confirmed that 9 out of 10 business advisers had personally run or managed a small business.[37] Barbara Roche MP stated her belief that the vast majority of advisers had "suffered all the anxieties that a small business manager has."[38] Academically, over 90 percent of advisers held a degree level qualification or higher.

In addition, each Business Link faced a contractual requirement to hold the Investors in People Standard. Staff development is mandatory under this scheme and each adviser was compelled to evidence at least 60 hours of training and professional development per annum. Continuous personal development was already part of the Business Link culture prior to the advent of national standards.

When surveyed the one stakeholder group who never seemed to have an issue with the quality were the customers themselves. An independent Ernst and Young survey of small and medium sized businesses concluded Business Link Advisers were "highly valued" by customers. Over 40 percent of customers believed it "unlikely that they could have got the same results by seeking help elsewhere."[39]

That is not to say there wasn't room for improvement. Customer satisfaction with the Business Link service stood at a fairly uninspiring 81 percent in 2001. This fairly immediate customer opinion was in spite of the inevitable delay in seeing returns accrue. The 2001 Business Link Tracker Survey confirmed that "impact of BL assistance on performance in around half of firms occurs more than two years after the assistance is provided."

In the interests of a fair appraisal of value, it is worth highlighting the method used to complete customer satisfaction surveys on Business Link. Each question had five standard responses, a neither nor option being the middle choice. Odd numbers of responses give the customer a neutral easy out, even numbers force businesses to make a positive or negative appraisal. Human nature dictates people naturally gravitate towards a centre option. The selected answer structure broke with best practice for customer survey. Positive feedback would only count if a small business scored the Business Link service "Satisfied" or "Very Satisfied." The easy to select middle option of neither nor was deemed a negative rating. This classfication system does put a slightly different perspective on customer satisfaction statistics for Business Links.

In the absence of any structured professional development from government (bar the SFEDI process), the individual Business Links implemented autonomous people development strategies. The lack of direction had exacerbated an ever increasing variation between regions and advisers. The closest the Business Links came to a shared approach to developing business advisers was the Forum 21 model. This private sector company delivered training to advisers through founder John McMahon. His principles were adopted widely by Business Links, covering over 40 percent of the network.[40] However, this methodology was not prescribed by government and it was up to each independent Business Link to decide how best to train advisers. When it came to people, Business Links could do what they will, so long as they all ensured customer facing staff could boast the "SFEDI patch."

Feeding the Myth

Business Links did not help themselves in the latter years by failing to promote their knowledgeable, if often outspoken, business adviser teams. For example, when Lord Sugar made his comment "to be perfectly frank, apart from meeting a nice bunch of people, there was no real business advice dished out other than simple stuff", he had recently visited the South West on a fact finding mission for the Government. At that time the Business Adviser team in Devon and Cornwall alone was "intensively" advising over 3,000 businesses face to face each year. These business owners were grading the service at 92 percent "satisfied" and "very satisfied." The adviser team had all recently completed the highly regarded Institute of Directors Certificate in Company Direction at Exeter University (over 90 percent pass rate). The majority of advisers also had experience of running their own business. You have to ask the question. At a sensitive time for contracts, how many of the vocal business advisers were introduced to Lord Sugar on his travels through Business Links?

It is true that the adviser team had shifted to a younger demographic in recent years. However, perhaps it was a risk worth taking in retrospect, particularly when the result was a public roasting in the press from the Government's Business Tsar.

Too Easy a Way

"If you set up an organisation like that, you are going to get a lot of criticism. You are going to get criticisms particularly about the people who you are using to give advice, because people will say they don't have any real experience, they don't have any real knowledge, and those are the people that will create the image in too easy a way."

The Rt Hon the Lord Heseltine CH

Interview with author at Haymarket Head Office, Hammersmith - 8th June, 2011

The key protaganists questioning the quality of people were the British Chambers of Commerce, the Federation of Small Businesses and Enterprise Agencies. Each of these organisations had a stake in the Business Link, be it as a formal partner, sub-contractor or peer. Each held a passionate belief that they knew best the needs of small businesses and were ever present voices influencing economic strategy in the United Kingdom. As private sector organisations they paid their own way using a mix of subscriptions and consultancy fees.

It is in this competitive climate that Business Link, an impartial and free form of business support, would operate. Any rivallry went right down to the coal face and, whilst there are examples of excellent collaborative working between Business Link advisers and these groups, there are an equal number of situations when barriers were put up. Almost certainly to the detriment of the customer who received less value.

On June 8th, 2011, the founder of Business Link, Lord Heseltine, shared his views on these groups and their relationships with the organisation.

- British Chambers of Commerce:

   "I think they regarded Business Link as an intrusion into their fiefdom. But the reason we created Business Link was because the Chambers weren't doing a good enough job. So there was a tension there from the beginning. They themselves should have set up this combined advisory service."

- Federation of Small Businesses:

   "Well they would be 'Get Off Our Backs' school of thinking. They would believe that small business doesn't need that sort of public advice. I don't agree with that particular judgement. The scale of the enquiries reveals that the demand was there. We can argue about whether the quality of the service was good enough. But my view would have been that could only lead to a debate about how you could improve it, not closing it down."

The Rt Hon the Lord Heseltine CH

Interview with author at Haymarket Head Office, Hammersmith - 8th June, 2011

Lord Heseltine made no judgement on Enterprise Agencies, except to confirm that these organisations "weren't a central part of what we were doing", which may go some way to explain why the criticism was most voracious from this quarter.

What is abundantly clear from the criticism is that government funded business support is not as simple as just helping small business. There are a number of agendas, all highly politicised, all believing zealously that their way is best.

Moving the Goalposts

In 1998, the Enhanced Vision for Business Links set out a vision to raise "quality, quality, quality" across the network. In a knowledge transfer business, the spotlight inevitably fell on the capability of the conduit, the Business Advisers. Business Link was not perfect, reacting to the frequently changing demands of their paymaster. Furthermore, advisers were human beings, each holding a unique mix of background, knowledge and experience. They would not always get it right.

On 2nd May, 2001, the Government confirmed a policy change with far reaching and serious impact on the value of the Business Link service, far greater than the National Standards and Business Link University combined.

"We have also changed the way advisers work so they will act far more as a facilitator with the client, far more as a process-consultant, working with clients to look at long-term objectives, identifying and putting together organisational development plans and bringing in the most appropriate expertise from wherever that exists, rather than necessarily trying to do everything directly themselves."

David Irwin – Chief Executive of the Small Business Service
Select Committee on Trade and Industry - Wednesday 2nd May, 2001.

This job brief made no mention of knowledge at all. Advisers in the future would be directed to keep hands off at all costs, and facilitate solutions instead. If you were a small business, in real terms, this meant that even when an adviser had the personal knowledge to help fix a problem, telling you the answer was against company policy.

If advisers followed the rules, you would no longer get the best of them. An era of strict information, diagnostic and brokerage (IDB) was dawning.

CHAPTER SEVEN

A SMALL BUSINESS SERVICE

2001

"The British Chambers of Commerce remarked to us that they were 'surprised to receive the first drafts of Small Business Service (SBS) contracts which focused very much on inputs, with page upon page of financial, operational and information requirements that would tie-up resource that should be customer-facing. This seemed inappropriate from an organisation that has the function of championing against red tape in Government'."

House of Commons Trade and Industry Committee
Thirteenth Report 9th May, 2001

The Labour Government launched the Small Business Service (SBS) as an Executive Agency on 3rd April, 2000. This new organisation was modelled broadly on the US Small Business Administration, an independent agency of the Federal Government whose role was to "aid, counsel, assist and protect the interests of small business concerns." The UK version had a similar remit.

"We will be a strong voice for small business at the heart of Government, ensuring that Government is aware of, and responsive to, the needs of all small businesses; to strive for a regulatory framework which minimises the burdens on business; to develop and maintain a world-class business support service to enhance businesses' competitiveness and profitability; and to champion the importance of entrepreneurship across society."

Nigel Griffiths - Minister for Small Business and Enterprise

Commons Debate - Written Answers to Questions:

Transport, Local Government and the Regions, 10th July, 2001

It's hard to see how this differed significantly from the visions set out previously by the Department of Trade and Industry, apart from the fact that for the first time all the Government's support for small businesses would be controlled by a single Agency, using Business Link as their main arm for delivery.

"The SBS is working with the regional development agencies to ensure a clear understanding of economic priorities and is committed to developing the Business Link network as the natural choice of smaller businesses seeking advice and support."

Patricia Hewitt, Secretary of State for Trade and Industry

Commons Debate - Written Answers to Questions:

Transport, Local Government and the Regions, 10th July, 2001

During 1999, "21 per cent of the Business Link hubs accounted for 40 per cent of those clients dissatisfied with services. Intensive services, particularly those delivered by Personal Business Advisers, achieved the highest satisfaction ratings."[41] The Government would no longer tolerate pockets of weakness or inconsistency across the new franchise.

"Some Business Link operators were very good and had a good reputation and their clients thought very highly of them, but I think it is fair to say that some did not quite meet those same standards of excellence. We were determined we should use the opportunity to try to raise the quality. We also think having a smaller number will ensure we have less resource in the back office, as it were, and far more happening in the front office, far greater customer focus."

David Irwin, CEO of the Small Business Service

House of Commons, Trade and Industry Minutes of Evidence 2nd May, 2001

SBS would actively police the new Business Links to ensure promises were delivered. They would not compromise on Business Links delivering the core suite of business support products in a consistent manner. There would be "room for manoeuvre" regarding searching out new sources of revenue and creating "local solutions for local needs." This freedom would create more enterprising Business Links but seemed at odds with reducing variability.

Irregular Contraction

Not surprisingly, despite the rather neutral tone of "rationalisation", this act was a practical process in pain for just about everyone involved. In less than 18 months the Business Link network was reduced from 80 independent partnerships to just 43 franchisees, covering 45 regions in England. The rationale for revolution rather than evolution was put squarely on the shoulders of small business.

"We heard some criticism of the absence of a clear national strategy for business support, the bureaucracy of the new contract regime, and the loss of commercial flexibility. There are general hopes that the refreshed network will have a clearer customer focus, and will benefit from its wider remit and the reduced number of outlets."

Patricia Hewitt, Secretary of State for Trade and Industry

House of Commons, Trade and Industry Minutes of Evidence 12 December ,2001

Franchise Prize

The franchisee application process was designed to be robust. Awarding bodies were deliberately loaded with owners and managers of small and medium sized businesses to ensure all the bids were subject to private sector scrutiny. All 80 existing Business Links were invited to apply for the new contracts. This round of bidding was closed and uncontested. No organisation outside the old network could enter a proposal.

Paper bids were submitted followed by a presentation to Regional Assessment Panels. The assessment panel awarded 32 of the new franchisee contracts at this first stage. The remaining 13 regions went out to open tender. The successful bidders were each awarded a three-year rolling Business Link contract.

These results could have attracted accusations of cosmetic exercise, as old Business Link partnerships won 72% of the new contracts, uncontested. However, each of these organisations had adapted to the new policies and endured a degree of pain to win the bids. For example, in Business Link Norfolk there was a reduction in directly employed personnel of 80 percent, over a period of three months. The Board sought to focus on brokerage not advice and became a "virtual" Business Link, staffed primarily by Contract Managers, an experiment predictably short-lived.

"The model was always an unusual franchise because rather than adopt a tried and tested business model, the franchisees were individual local partnerships."

Economic Impact Study of Business Link Local Service - Project Report

Department for Business Enterprise and Regulatory Reform (BERR)

Saal, D; Mole, K; Roper, S and Hart, M (2006)

One of the primary objectives of the Business Link rationalisation was to inject a degree of consistency into the Business Link network. Research by Bennett and Robson in 2003 suggested the new Business Links were not as independent as hoped.[42] Only 26 of the 43 franchisees were deemed to be "truly independent", 4 were subsidiaries, 11 were "de facto subsidiaries" of Chambers of Commerce, and just 2 were for profit companies.

In addition, there was still no dictat on how the franchisees should operate, as autonomy at local level remained a priority, just as it had in 1994, when Conservatives ran Business Link. Directors of the franchisee organisations had different steers on how they wanted to develop their organisations. This combination of different Board direction and the freedom to innovate services in the regions did nothing to eliminate inconsistency. Rather this structure embedded a degree of postcode lottery into the network.

In 2006, an Economic Impact Study suggested four very different business models could be found in the new Business Link network.[43]

Thirty franchisees had committed to a "light-touch brokerage" model serving as many small and medium sized business customers as possible. With a limited increase in resources these organisations tried to solve business problems on the spot and were no longer in a position to provide meaningful follow up.

Eight Business Links had opted for a "managed brokerage" business model. These franchisees were committed to project managing relationships with consultants from start to finish. Their resources were focused on supporting a select number of growth businesses more intensively.

Six Business Links chose to use "pipeline forcing" strategies by filtering carefully who received the Business Link service. Once these select growth businesses were signed up, the franchisees persuaded these clients to stay on board for the long haul, at least until the support was fully completed.

Whatever the selected business model, 70 percent of Business Links had implemented a sales and marketing strategy based on serving as many customers as possible, market 'penetration' being a key performance indicator for the SBS. The minority had actually committed to deploying their adviser team in a knowledge centred way, working exclusively with a select band of growth clients. These organisations were focused on the other key performance indicator for the SBS, customer satisfaction.

Now, more than ever, where a small business office was located would dictate how much support was on offer.

Baked Beans

The most striking change resulting from the Small Business Service takeover was the culture shift towards performance management. Prior to 1997, the brief for a business adviser had been simplistic in the extreme.

"We wanted a team of people who could hold their hand, listen to their problems, have a working knowledge of what business is about, to make suggestions, to ask questions, become a friend in need. What the form of the questions were and what the opportunities of dialogue would unfold, that was never prescriptive. We never tried to tell anyone how to conduct an interview or what to look for."

The Rt Hon the Lord Heseltine CH

Interview with author at Haymarket Head Office, Hammersmith - 8th June, 2011

Prior to the Small Business Service, Business Link performance was judged primarily on how happy customers felt about the service i.e. the contribution small businesses perceived the intervention had made to bottom line performance.

The Small Business Service (SBS) was an Executive Agency of the Government and obligated to report performance regularly to Parliament. As a result, Business Links were ordered to supply management information to counter the ever-increasing scrutiny over the SBS budget. The SBS decreed a number of key performance indicators (KPI) to *prove* Business Links were helping.

KPI 1 – Penetration

In 2001, David Irwin, Chief Executive of the Small Business Service, suggested market penetration for businesses employing over fifty persons was just fewer than 50 percent, whereas for businesses employing less than ten it was 3 percent. When Labour took over in 1997, the Business Links were under fairly sustained attack for helping a small select group of businesses, those that had high growth potential. These accusations seem at odds with the vision of Business Link founder Lord Heseltine. When asked in 2011 about helping businesses with over £250,000 turnover, Lord Heseltine stated "a lot of the advice I would have imagined at the early stage would have gone to people employing 2 to 5 people."[44]

Whatever the reality, the demand for market penetration was to become an obsession for the Small Business Service. This measure would be key ammunition to fend off any accusations of minority impact.

"One of the key changes in the specification we have for the new Business Link network as opposed to its predecessor is that they should explicitly promote themselves as offering services to all businesses rather than concentrating on those larger businesses with growth potential. So we would expect to see some change in the balance."

Hâf Merrifield, Director of Local Network Development (SBS)
House of Commons, Trade and Industry Minutes of Evidence 2nd May, 2001

In 2003, the SBS reported the number of organisations helped by Business Link had doubled in a single year, rising from 150,000 to 300,000 small businesses.[45] The Business Link budgets and numbers in the adviser team did not increase by the same proportion. Business Links were forced to machine through the required numbers and the emphasis was inevitably switched to lower cost ways of achieving volume support, including telephone advice, day clinics and seminars.

KPI 2 – The Hay Day of GVA

"The Small Business Service has introduced a Gross Value Added measure as part of its Performance Management Framework for Business Link. This enables operators to quantify the impact they have had on businesses with which they have formed a more intensive relationship, in terms of wealth creation and productivity improvement."

Nigel Griffiths MP - Parliamentary Under Secretary of State at the Department of

Trade and Industry

House of Commons Debates, Written Answers to Questions 20 January, 2004

The Government needed hard evidence that return on investment was being generated for the taxpayer, not a long list of small and medium sized businesses smiling. Customer satisfaction just wouldn't cut the mustard in a Tony Blair era of league tables. Small businesses clearly couldn't be trusted to give a fair and balanced opinion. Numbers would speak much louder than words.

Gross value added is a new concept for most small and medium sized businesses, indeed most business advisers wouldn't even try to explain it. The technical measure is profits plus payroll and depreciation costs. This approach had the added benefit of using figures from a profit and loss account and not a balance sheet (which many small businesses are unable to provide). These figures were like nectar to the gods for government. Small business profits were injected back into the economy and payroll was money put in employees' pockets to spend. If the Government was willing to give small business a tax-funded service, this was the way they would measure return on investment. Simple enough for any basic accountant to put together but what was the practical relevance to a small and medium sized business, if any?

The majority of small and medium sized businesses do not measure depreciation day to day, the figure typically being something the accountant produces at the end of the financial year to reduce tax burden. The majority of small business owners do not understand how it is calculated or why it matters. Obtaining estimates often entailed speaking to an accountant. As a result, collection of the data itself was not straight forward, as illustrated by the Aston Business School, professional researchers collecting market data.

"Our attempts at collecting value added data from BL clients as part of the telephone survey proved ineffective yielding low response rates. It did prove possible, however, to obtain high response rates for turnover and employment growth in the survey and we have therefore used these figures in the modelling work."

Economic Impact Study of Business Link Local Service - Project Report

Department for Business Enterprise and Regulatory Reform (BERR)

Saal, D; Mole, K; Roper, S and Hart, M (2006)

Practicalities aside, the most difficult issue with GVA would be determining contribution. It would be ludicrous to claim an adviser was responsible for 100% of any business' growth. Conversely, Business Links were equally not 100% responsible if a small business cocked it all up. Adviser input may have been important regarding stimulating strategy and ideas, but the business makes it all happen and puts in the effort, finance and management. The adviser was more catalyst than conductor, as at their best they would probably spend a maximum of ten days per annum working with a client.

The Business Link University spent time exploring contribution and as I recall, their findings estimated at best 20% of any improvement could be directly attributed to the actions of the adviser. On what scientific basis is anyone's guess when every situation is so unique. After working with over 1,000 small businesses, the author believes this figure is a fair assessment. Certainly no more than this amount. If any higher then the business adviser activity should probably be classified as consultancy and displacement of existing business support services. It was a fine line.

From the perspective of a small business, they didn't care who took the credit, as long as the bank balance went in the right direction.

On the plus side, at least GVA embedded ownership of small business issues into the adviser mindset. The customer's financial growth was now a key performance objective for each adviser, subject to formal appraisal by management. However, from a Business Link standpoint, GVA was an additional drain on resources. The collection, recording and recollection (one year on) of these figures would be an administrative burden that added virtually zero value for small businesses in this country. Advisers were now spending time counting when they could have been helping small businesses improve performance.

Regardless, the SBS was more than satisfied. These figures justified their existence (and Business Links) to politicians and critics alike.

KPI 3 – Customer Sat

Customer satisfaction was the third headline measure imposed by the SBS on Business Link. The opinions of small businesses were still important. This information would provide useful market research for the Business Links and serve as an effective sound bite to counter any accusations that customers were unhappy. The Small Business Service appointed independent contractors from the private sector to complete the customer surveys and prevent any accusations of bias.

Once again, with enthusiastic performance monitoring, the SBS ensured Business Links increased recorded customer satisfaction.

"In 2002, customer satisfaction with Business Link Operator services increased to 84 percent from 81 percent. By the end of quarter two 2003–04, the provisional average customer satisfaction rate of 85.4 per cent shows a 1 percent increase on the last six months and a 3.2 per cent increase on the same period last year."

Nigel Griffiths MP - Parliamentary Under Secretary of State at the Department of Trade and Industry
House of Commons Debates, Written Answers to Questions 20 January, 2004

As for meaningful results, small and medium sized businesses were always surveyed one to three months after meeting their adviser.

However, the majority of customers accrued returns after a period of 12 months (since the Business Link intervention).[46] Based on these findings, was this fairly immediate survey measuring quality of service rather than value added to the business?

Points Mean Prizes

"The Small Business Service (SBS) has developed a core set of key performance indicators (KPIs) to measure the success and effectiveness of Business Link Operators (BLOs). These indicators are contained in a Performance Management Framework and reflect the performance, value and contribution to the economy made by BLOs."

Nigel Griffiths MP - Parliamentary Under Secretary of State at the Department of

Trade and Industry

House of Commons Debates, Written Answers to Questions 20 January, 2004

On 1st April, 2001, the SBS assumed direct management responsibility for the 43 new Business Link organisations. From the outset the Small Business Service imposed a strict measurement culture on the Business Links to control performance and inconsistency in the network. Each year the 43 Business Links had to agree an annual Delivery Plan with the SBS. These plans were based on achieving a standard set of key performance measures, common to every contract. The three contractual key performance measures were:

• Penetration – number of users accessing Business Link service

• Intensively assisted businesses (adviser team)

• Customer satisfaction

These targets were then supplemented by a number of secondary measures.

- Awareness of Business Link (prompted and unprompted)

- Understanding of Business Link services

- Financial efficiency (of individual Business Links)

- Perceived business benefit

- Changes in Gross Value Added of Business Link customers

The Small Business Service would vigorously monitor and review performance of each Business Link on a quarterly basis. Each Business Link would be subject to an annual independent audit of their finances and management information systems. The SBS was determined all their money would be spent as intended. If these targets were not being met the SBS reserved the right to take corrective action. This threat would not be an idle one.

Corrective Measures

Operationally, the Small Business Service had put eight Business Links into corrective measures by the end of 2003. BL Derbyshire, BL Tees Valley, BL Bedfordshire and Luton were categorised as "seriously under performing" and did not have their contracts automatically renewed. BL Derbyshire's market penetration had fallen from 15.5 to 12.2 percent in less than 12 months, and their customer satisfaction had fallen from 83.1 to 76 percent. On the other hand, BL Tees Valley had a strong market penetration at 25.1 percent but an alarm-ringing customer satisfaction rating of 71.3 percent. Cambridge Business Services and Sussex Enterprise were classified as "under performing, but to a less serious extent." This meant their Business Link contract was renewed but an immediate full business performance review would be needed to retain active status. BL Leicestershire, BL Northamptonshire Chamber Business Enterprise (Manchester) and BL South Yorkshire were also asked to complete formal business reviews.[47]

More seriously, on 6th February, 2004, Nigel Griffiths confirmed in the House of Commons that the independent auditors had "identified serious weaknesses in a Business Link's financial and management systems." This example was the only case of financial irregularity uncovered between 1997 and 2005. The Business Link concerned was forced to complete a Business Performance Review and to take remedial action before their contract would be renewed.

After all of the reviews were completed and remedial action taken, none of the Business Links actually had their contract withdrawn. Each organisation received a new mandate from the Small Business Service for another three years. Not a single player received a red card.

The Small Business Service had shown willingness to take corrective action and the prospect of being named and shamed, not to mention the operational and financial disruption, bred a near obsession for numbers at any cost within Business Link management. This philosophy was frequently at odds with the business adviser team.

Whilst it is easy for managers to get carried away with graphs and spreadsheets, advisers did not have quite the same luxury. They had no choice but to look into the whites of the eyes of small business owners. Faced with the stark reality in the field that business is about people not numbers, advisers inevitably tried to ensure small businesses received the help they needed. For this reason alone it would always be customer first, company second for the majority of advisers. This would be an uncomfortable truth for any employer.

Turbulence and Pain

"The SBS took over in the regions from Business Link in April 2001: There has been a major shake out of the BL network. The new structure is based on a contract, with each BL run privately and offering franchised services overseen by the SBS. The process has been *turbulent* in some areas."

House of Commons Trade and Industry Committee
Thirteenth Report 9th May ,2001

The process of rationalisation had not been as straightforward as hoped and the Small Business Service had been forced to acknowledge a number of failings when challenged by the Trade and Industry Committee.

Firstly the Small Business Service confirmed they had seriously underestimated the length of time it would take to agree contracts for Business Links. As mentioned previously, each existing Business Link partnership was unique in both structure and degree of experience. The fact a number of bidding organisations were unready for complex negotiations came as a surprise. Indeed, the Small Business Service itself admitted handholding a number of bidders through the process. David Irwin, Chief Executive of the Small Business Service told the Committee "we have learnt that perhaps we should have devoted a bit more time and started a bit earlier with some of the contracting."[48] To compound the situation, as with any downsizing process, the people complexity in terms of redundancy and Transfer of Undertakings (Protection of Employment) Regulations (TUPE) for each bidding organisation was both significant and painful. The change of business model caused a relative culture shock, shifting overnight to market penetration and facilitation, rather than direct hands on support, albeit the reduced emphasis on fees was a welcome change. The legacy personnel, retained by the successful bidding organisations, had been recruited based on their experience and consultancy knowledge. These skills did not necessarily suit the new role for advisers.

Finally, by his own admission, the leader of the Small Business Service was new to dealing with the politics and sensitivities of government.

"Perhaps I should also explain that I have come in from an outside organisation, so not only is the organisation new but I am new as well. I am not a civil servant, I have come in from an Enterprise Agency, so I have been having to learn a lot about both how the Civil Service works and how Government funding works."

David Irwin, Chief Executive of the Small Business Service
House of Commons Trade and Industry Minutes of Evidence 2nd May, 2001

Mr Irwin did not seek reappointment at the end of his two years contract. On 12th December, 2001, Patricia Hewitt, Secretary for Trade and Industry, told the Trade and Industry Committee that his role had been "vitally important" in creating the Small Business Service and "putting in place the new framework of Business Links." She went on to acknowledge "I think it is very difficult for a civil servant, and David Irwin became a civil servant, to fulfil the role of being a strong voice for small business on the issue of regulation."[49]

David Irwin had co-founded Project North East in 1980. As Director he steered this innovative economic development agency to an annual turnover exceeding £4 million by 2000.[50] In anyone's book, David Irwin was a successful entrepreneur when he joined the Small Business Service. A business owner recruited to set up and run the Small Business Service. Did the challenge of running a government agency have anything to do with entrepreneurial capability?

Whatever the answer, the final word on the Small Business Service goes to David Irwin himself.

"Has the transition from the old Business Link system been a painful experience? Hâf (Merrifield) is nodding, so it must have been. It is fair to say that the system had a lot of conflicting demands made of it over a comparatively short period."

David Irwin, Chief Executive of the Small Business Service
House of Commons Trade and Industry Minutes of Evidence 2nd May, 2001

Far from being growing pains, in the future the 43 new Business Links would have to accept conflicting demands as the one constant from government.

Sudden Impact

The Small Business Service could be accused of diluting the value per customer at the coalface, but their ability to engineer improvement in key performance indicators was undeniable.

Existing Business (not start up)	Market Penetration	Customer Satisfaction
2001 – 2002	245,342 (14%)	81%
2002 – 2003	309,665 (17%)	84%
2003 – 2004	435,293 (24%)	86%

Market penetration percentage is against the Inter-Departmental Business Register total for each respective year.

Sources of table data: House of Commons Hansard Written Answers for 21 Jul 2004

The Small Business Service was proud of their performance and linked this directly to the Business Links rationalisation.

"In terms of the outcomes from the investment of rationalising the old Business Link network of more than four years ago from 83 operating companies down to 45, despite the disruption in doing that in and around 2000, I think we have come out the other side with some good impacts."

Mr Martin Wyn Griffith, Chief Executive of the Small Business Service

House of Commons Trade and Industry Minutes of Evidence 6th January, 2004

This hike in the key performance indicators is all the more remarkable when you consider budgets for the Business Link network remained unchanged in real terms. In the financial year ending April 2004, the Small Business Service allocated £139.5 million of core funding to the 43 Business Links. From 1999 to 2000, the year before the Small Business Service takeover, investment in the Business Link network was £120 million, equivalent to £131.5 million in 2004. So without a huge hike in investment, how were these improvements being achieved? Had rationalisation really improved customer focus and diverted more resources to front line services, as former SBS Chief Executive David Irwin had hoped?

It is difficult to challenge the numbers, which would have been subject to audit. The majority of Business Links had undoubtedly evolved into efficient lighter touch machines, quickly in, quickly out and leave some value. More businesses were indeed getting a piece of the tax payer pie. However, it should be noted that rapid growth was achieved with a corresponding investment in sales and marketing.

This promotional use of taxpayer funds was off the radar to the general public, but repeatedly challenged in the House of Commons and in Committee by members of the Opposition. In July 2002, Patricia Hewitt confirmed the Small Business Service had invested £6,630,590 in the previous financial year on advertising expenditure. Raising Business Link awareness alone cost £2,450,781. From 1998 to 1999, the cost of advertising had been £1,021,352.[53]

The Small Business Service invested additional funding for delivery of specialist advisory programmes such as UK Online for Business, Local Partnership Fund and High Growth Start-up. These initiatives were rolled out under the Business Link banner during the reign of the Small Business Service. This surplus activity provided an additional boost to penetration, with 170,749 pre-starts being served in 2003. Similarly, these new schemes needed promotional expense to succeed. During 2002 to 2003, the Department of Trade and Industry spent £2,883,832 advertising the UK Online for Business scheme alone. Reaching out to the masses comes at a price.

Intensive Care

In 2002, the Cambridge Business Research survey concluded that Business Link was the "foremost single source of public sector business support." Despite this achievement, the same research reaffirmed the direct linkage between the "characteristics of the individual adviser" and customer satisfaction levels.

By design the Small Business Service had limited the impact an adviser could make directly in a small business. Yet, even working just as facilitator, the adviser's personal experience and expertise still determined the value for a customer.

The Economic Impact Study of Business Link Local Service (2006) estimated that during a six months period in 2003 over £750 million value was added to small and medium sized businesses using "intensive" services. This figure is five times the cost of Business Link at the time. Two out of three "intensively assisted" customers went on to credit Business Link as "the crucial factor in levering behavioural change within the firm."

The Business Link advisory team remained crucial to the Small Business Service (SBS), if they were going to hit their value target for Government. As early as 1999, a Bennett and Robson report had recommended the agency "focus on increasing intensity of support" for those clients that need it. However, the SBS was ultimately tasked to raise market penetration and deliver consistency across the Business Link network. Launched within Business Links in 2004, Support to Implement Best Business Practice (Product 10) would be the boldest attempt yet to standardise the advisory process and ensure every growth business shared a similar experience.

Benchmarking was back.

CHAPTER EIGHT

BEST IN CLASS

2004

"The diagnostic represents an opportunity for your business to take an objective view of its performance, allowing you to look at the performance of other companies and determining not only what is possible (best in class) but also what is critical for you to compete effectively in your chosen market. It will quickly and intuitively highlight specific areas of improvement and change and encourage you to make decisions that are based on facts, not just intuition or hunch."

Support to Implement Best Business Practice
Core Diagnostic Questionnaire 2004

On 1st April, 2004, the Department of Trade and Industry launched Support to Implement Best Business Practice (SIBBP). This initiative was part of the significantly reduced range of services available to small and medium sized businesses, nine repackaged "products" to simplify access for small and medium sized business.

<u>Succeeding Through Innovation:</u>

1. Knowledge Transfer Networks
2. Collaborative research and development
3. Grant for investigating an innovative idea
4. Grant for research and development
5. Knowledge Transfer Partnership

<u>Raising Finance:</u>

6. Small Firms Loan Guarantee

<u>Regional Investment:</u>

7. Selective Finance for Investment in England

<u>Achieving Best Practice in your Business:</u>

8. Access to Best Business Practice
9. Support to Implement Best Business Practice (SIBBP)

Note: Whilst Support to Implement Best Business Practice continued to be widely known as Product 10, the Department of Trade and Industry had merged two of the original initiatives into one, removing this tenth listing.

The Best Practice products would be a flagship element of the Business Link service for the next 12 months, having a significant impact on the advisory process and forcing benchmarking firmly back on the agenda.

In 2001, the Small Business Service had shifted the role of the business adviser to emphasise brokerage and referral rather than direct help. However, the adviser still possessed a significant amount of influence over what happened at the coalface, being the face of Business Link and reacting directly to customers needs. The Department of Trade and Industry believed a more process driven approach to diagnosis would increase consistency across the network and ensure businesses received a similar health check, regardless of whom your 'GP' might be. The Government was determined to eliminate any maverick behaviour by advisers.

Snow to the Eskimo

The strength of the Business Link model was *no* hard sell to muddy the waters. As a result, the advisers' agenda was simply to act in the best interests of small businesses, to be honest and not to sell something the customer didn't need. Most advisers were loyal to this core value, recognising that the relationship would be terminally damaged by inappropriate (and risky) referrals. The degree of referrals to consultants would always be a desirable requirement, rather than a contractual target. However, after 2004, a percentage for the amount of brokerage expected was communicated to staff. This figure was driven primarily from two sources.

The Small Business Service (and subsequently Regional Development Agencies) demanded to see evidence of brokerage from advisers, to prove they were stimulating the market as intended. Secondly, the individual Business Links frequently had other contracts outside the Business Link franchise, e.g. income generating targets for apprentices and environmental support. That these numbers were reached was critical to meet the contractual requirements and maintain the extra income needed to finance Business Link organisations.

This inherent conflict of interest created a degree of tension between the adviser team and management. On the one hand, the message was never do anything to compromise customers and retain complete autonomy regarding recommendations. On the other, the implied directive was get out there and sell these products to customers.

In my experience, the vast majority of advisers would rather miss their personal targets than recommend anything that wasn't 100% right, in both timing and substance, for a small business customer.

Broken Broker?

"The implementation of brokerage has spawned more than one model, including 'internal' brokerage where there is modest independence between the broker and client. Bryson (1997) argued that advisers would be more likely to work with consultants with whom they have worked previously leading to favouritism and a joint dependency."

Economic Impact Study of Business Link Local Service - Project Report

Department for Business Enterprise and Regulatory Reform (BERR)

Saal, D; Mole, K; Roper, S and Hart, M (2006)

The Small Business Service (SBS) insisted on a transparent and impartial audit trail to ensure advisers were not steering the selection of external consultants. If advisers could decide *who* was best for a small business, as well as *what*, this could create a number of weaknesses and threats for Business Link. Advisers inevitably develop personal relationships with customers. This emotional attachment, however small, could influence their judgement when selecting the suppliers, matching people to people, rather than need to solution. In knowledge transfer, it is imperative the two parties get along and understand each other to be productive, both soft measures.

In addition, an adviser may have limited knowledge of suppliers in the market place, particularly if they are new recruits. A tendency may develop where the adviser relies on a small number of consultants known to them personally, who in their personal judgement, deliver the required value for small and medium sized businesses. This approach leads to a relatively narrow view of the knowledge available (limiting what could have been achieved). It is also in conflict with the Business Link ethos, to stimulate consultancy and be impartial. However, human nature dictates people naturally steer away from risk and want to retain control of the process. It is this premise that opened the network up to accusations of 'black books' and the 'back-hander'. Personally, I never witnessed any adviser act without integrity and in the best interests of customers. That isn't to say categorically this didn't happen on occasion. Finally, advisers may be constrained by a public sector culture offering a finite portfolio of support "products", schemes to be promoted to small and medium sized businesses over alternative solutions in the private sector. When it came to small business customers, internal brokerage was of course far more prevalent than external referrals. The Business Link adviser referred small businesses to colleagues and other subsidised business support providers, usually because these were free to access and good quality. It was a safer choice for a more limited budget.

"Once subsidy ends former Business Link clients are more likely to seek further external advice. More surprising perhaps is that only 51.7 per cent of intensively assisted firms reported paying for externally referred services. Therefore, considerable external brokering by Business Link staff was to non-fee paying services rather than market based services."

Economic Impact Study of Business Link Local Service - Project Report

Department for Business Enterprise and Regulatory Reform (BERR)

Saal, D; Mole, K; Roper, S and Hart, M (2006)

In reality, the main barrier to brokerage activity was propensity and ability to pay. If you are working with small businesses, cash is tight. A fact rarely recognised by target setters. If the Business Links really were intended to help small and medium sized businesses, does making the customer pay for something you know is free elsewhere really make a positive contribution? Robbing from Peter to please Paul? Whether such schemes should have been free in the first place is another argument.

More Winning Moves

In 2003, Department of Trade and Industry (DTI) policy remained firmly committed to helping businesses implement best business practice. Private sector contractor Winning Moves was appointed to develop a new best practice programme (with their existing Benchmark Index service at it's core). The two resulting products would be tailored to the needs of organisations employing between 10 and 200 employees, rather than bigger business.

Access to Best Business Practice (ABBP)

The company Winning Moves was tasked with creating a suite of business guides, all focused on spreading best practice using simple to understand, high value information. The resulting ABBP library featured original material in key areas of business competitiveness. These documents included:

Management:

- Ideas for Business Management
- Best Companies: Best Practice
- Accountancy Services – a guide to best practice

Sales and Marketing:

- E-Marketing
- Building an E-Commerce Website
- Information Security

Operations:

- Quality Management
- Technology, Customers and Suppliers: Supply Chain
- Quality, Cost and Delivery: Measuring Manufacturing Performance

People:

- Maximising Potential: High Performance Workplaces
- Work Life Balance and Flexible Working – the Business Case
- Building your Business' Skills and Capabilities

Communications and IT:

- Mobile Working
- Broadband
- BS 7799 and the Data Protection Act

Accessing information is not the same as consuming it. In a reactive system such as ABBP there was little opportunity to check the actual value created. However, initial demand for the service was more than encouraging.

"From 1 April, 2004, to 31 October, 2004, there have been over 300,000 visits to the Access to Best Practice pages on the DTI's website. During this period 100,000 hard copy publications have been ordered and dispatched. In October alone there were 50,000 downloads of electronic documents from the site. There are over 300 downloadable documents on the website covering aspects of business best practice as well as case studies."

Mr Nigel Griffiths MP, Parliamentary Under-Secretary at Department of Trade and Industry Commons Debates, Written Answers to Questions – 7th December, 2004

The shear scale of this project demanded a significant investment of taxpayer funds. On 18th November, 2004, Nigel Griffiths confirmed £6 million would be spent on ABBP in that financial year.[54] Whatever the final cost, this initiative was a significant influence on the delivery of future business support, moving towards automated advisory services. Best practice content, delivered online, transformed the Business Link / DTI websites and appeared to vindicate the opinion that self-serve support was the future. A huge volume of online transactions sealed the demise of the Business Link

Advisory Service, which was deemed no longer fit for purpose by 2011.

Support to Implement Best Business Practice (SIBBP / 'Product 10')

Not the catchiest name ever devised for a business support scheme. However, behind the rather uninspiring title laid a very significant intervention. Winning Moves had started product development using their 1990s DTI scheme, the Benchmark Index. The company transformed the Benchmark Index into a step-by-step process for advisers to follow. This preferred way of analysing an organisation was the first attempt in the history of Business Link to impose a process driven approach to diagnosis.

The DTI planned to push 10,000 growth businesses through the programme. However, the use of SIBBP was never a contractual condition, if only because it was impractical and probably unnecessary to apply in every micro business environment (businesses employing less than 10). Instead, Business Link operators were given a carrot and a stick to encourage take up of SIBBP within their advisory teams.

Each and every Personal Business Adviser in the Business Links network was trained in the SIBBP process. In practical terms, this involved sending 600 business advisers for three days of training (off site) in 2004 and a further 400 on benchmarking training a year later (when the product was revised and renamed Business Performance Diagnostic). A £5,000 consultancy grant was made available to every business going through the process. This sum was an incentive to organisations to give up their time and taste the benefits of best practice. However, it was also a significant lever to ensure advisers adopted the process as their own. In cash strapped small and medium sized businesses, accessing finance was always a priority. Finally, for every completed benchmark, the Business Link Operator concerned received an additional payment of £500 per customer.

Failure to meet the usage levels (even though these were not contractual targets) resulted in a reallocation of resources amongst the network. Or in plain language, if a Business Link didn't deliver the

DTI would give the budget to someone who would. This threat was actually followed through, a move that came as a nasty surprise to a number of under performing Business Link Operators.

Best Practitioner

The SIBBP process was not rocket science by any means. To experienced advisers there appeared similarities with existing business improvement methodology such as the Balanced Scorecard. To their credit, Winning Moves had resisted reinventing the wheel completely and creating complex labyrinths for an adviser to follow. Instead, the organisation had set out a step-by-step process based on proven management theory. Albeit the scheme tied the DTI into Winning Move's one unique asset, the data held within the Benchmark Index.

Operationally, the process was estimated to take four to five working days to complete. The Business Link adviser would do the bulk of the interpretation and administration. The cost to small businesses would be time alone.

Step 1 - Data Mining

The first step in the process was to complete a benchmark survey. Whilst the SIBBP questionnaire was a slimmed down version of the full Benchmark Index, it was still a daunting task for most small and medium sized businesses with fairly simple (if any) management information systems. Accountants were invariably called in to deliver up some numbers to complete the questionnaire.

The Core Module questionnaire had a total of 75 questions, although it was never mandatory to answer all the questions. However, whilst no policy on data collection was formally enforced, it was communicated clearly to advisers that a minimum number of answers were needed to make this a worthwhile process for everyone involved.

The questionnaire was designed to examine performance across an entire business:

Financial Data (27 questions)

- Financial revenue, management and costs including depreciation, research and development expenditure and marketing spend).

ICT expenditure (5 questions)

Processes (5 questions)

Customer satisfaction (7 questions)

Product or service innovation (6 questions)

Suppliers (3 questions)

People management (16 questions)

People satisfaction (6 questions)

Being able to answer all the questions was extremely rare, although undoubtedly this produced a higher quality analysis. The challenge of collecting accurate data on this scale was a deterrent to many small and medium sized businesses. Even if a business did have access to this quantity of management information (which was unlikely), the time involved made them think twice. As a result, most submissions of benchmark data were partially completed, devaluing the subsequent comparison and main benefit of benchmarking.

One benefit, not recorded for SIBBP, but very real never the less, was highlighting an inability to even get started. Introducing the process to a business starkly demonstrated how poorly a number of businesses used and valued management information. It is a very uncomfortable experience to be unable to answer simple questions about finance and performance on your own business. This was an epiphany moment for many.

Step 2 – Bench Press

The information supplied was inputted anonymously into the Benchmark database. A comparison report was then generated. This should have allowed a business to compare performance within set peer to peer groups, e.g. sector (competition), company size. The results would enable a "best in class" evaluation of performance, rather than a generic fairly meaningless comparison to the wider business community. Businesses are only creating competitive advantage if they improve *faster* than competitors.

In practice, the results were only as good as the number of other data sets available for comparison. At the launch of the project there was a relatively small number of benchmarks in the database, with clusters in particular sectors. For example, in 2002, the sister project Benchmark Index held 20% of data sets in the transport sector alone. Only 35.9% of the businesses that were benchmarked had less than £1 million sales.[55] Setting aside the issue of whether the data provided was accurate in the first place!

"Inaccurate answers will lead to erroneous results and will limit the value for your business."

Support to Implement Best Business Practice
Core Diagnostic Questionnaire 2004

Benchmarking would always be an imperfect science never intended to be black and white. However, the resulting report did suggest strengths and weaknesses compared against the competition, an in-sector comparison, which is as good a place as any to start a discussion.

Step 3 – Evaluation and Analysis

"The adviser's role is to question and to facilitate the development of the thinking in the owner's mind: 'Maybe I am missing out on an opportunity through which I could develop my business'. From a business adviser point of view you do not need a trained accountant to help a business with its finance issues. What you do need is someone who understands enough about managing a business to see that there is a cash flow problem and it might be about time to go and do something about that problem."

Mr Martin Wyn Griffith, Chief Executive of the Small Business Service
House of Commons Trade and Industry, Minutes of Evidence 6 January, 2004

Even with a process driven diagnostic tool, the knowledge of the adviser remained directly linked to amount of value added.

"It is not enough to know what your malaise is if you are not prescribed the right medicine, and indeed you haven't the commitment to take it."

Closing the Gap 3 (DTI Business Link and Cranfield University)
Neely, A.; Szwejczewski, M.; Jarrar, Y. - 20th September, 2002

The benchmark report highlighted variances against competitors, but it was still down to your adviser to help interpret these findings and recommend solutions.

"Invest your resources where they're most needed to add value to operations and manage performance. Achieve your business goals. Measure your progression towards achieving your aims and aspirations and keep yourself on track to get there. Encourage your business to S-t-r-e-t-c-h."

Benchmark Index - summary brochure
Winning Moves: www.winningmoves.com - 2011

"Stretch" was the buzzword from the Government in 2004 and at the heart of the SIBBP philosophy. The Government believed businesses should be setting targets well beyond their comfort zone to accelerate performance. Specific, Measurable, Achievable, Realistic and Time bound (SMART) targets just didn't stretch enough.

Step 4 – Call to Action

"Based on the results of this evaluation and analysis, in consultation with you, the adviser creates a practical, detailed action plan for your business that identifies key areas for improvement and highlights potential sources of help. In many cases the necessary changes are best made by the businesses themselves. Alternatively, your Business Link adviser might recommend a tailored implementation project for your business."

Support to Implement Best Business Practice

Core Diagnostic Questionnaire 2004

SIBBP had been launched in April 2004. By December, the Personal Business Advisers had completed 1,956 benchmarks with customers. The popularity of the new product appeared to differ depending on region. The South West contributed 18% of the entire total (339 organisations), whilst East Midlands had completed just 5% of benchmarks. The North East reported a total of 12 diagnostics in eight months.[56]

The output of the process was a tailored action plan focusing on three or four key failings and opportunities, highlighted during the benchmarking process. The Government expected projects to be brokered to external consultants who could work hands on with the small business to implement any solutions.

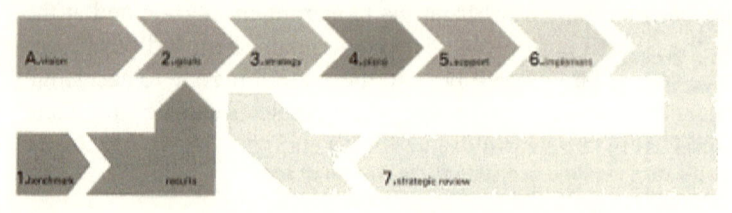

Finding your way around the document

Throughout this document you will see that each phase of the Business Performance Diagnostic is represented by a numbered block, the blocks being coloured to correspond with the phase of the diagnostic model to which each page refers (all other phases being shown in grey). The example shown here indicates that you are in the section that deals with the fourth phase (i.e: the creation of the Strategic Improvement Plan).

A develop the initial vision and goals

- get the client to identify aspirations for the future
- get the client to express these aspirations in the form of an initial vision and goals

1 undertake the diagnostic

- capture current performance data
- benchmark against selected comparison group to produce output report and then interrogate findings
- identify performance strengths and weaknesses

2 refine/reframe the goals

- introduce the diagnostic results
- validate vision & goals based on results – ensure vision is "compelling yet realisable" and goals are "ambitious yet achievable"
- re-state the goals and objectives

3 identify the priorities and improvement strategy

- brainstorm the key drivers and blockers to goal achievement
- develop ideas/strategies to achieve the objectives
- agree the priorities
- create a strategic framework for improvement aligned to each objective

Business Performance Diagnostic – A Toolkit for Advisers (Benchmark Process)
Published 2005 by Winning Moves Ltd

4 create the strategic improvement plan

- identify resources, accountabilities, timings, milestones and deliverables (reflecting the priorities previously agreed)
- create the action plan and commit to action

5 produce the support specification

- from the plan identify external support provisions
- align each support requirement with the objectives

6 implementation

- reflecting on the plan and support specification, undertake a sanity check to ensure that the plan is both coherent and deliverable
- using the Strategic Action Plan identify the first project to be executed
- investigate and identify available funding or grants to support the project
- provide the data required to enable the brokerage of suitable external specialists
- manage the external specialists in line with local Business Link policy
- repeat above steps for each of the other projects identified in the Strategic Action Plan

7 conduct the strategic review

- between 12-18 months after the brokerage, undertake a second Business Performance Diagnostic
- identify performance improvements and the impact of the brokerage
- revisit the client goals and set new horizons based on revised performance expectations

Business Performance Diagnostic – A Toolkit for Advisers (Benchmark Process)
Published 2005 by Winning Moves Ltd

"Significant assistance would be where we would be engaging with that business for three or four days, brokering in a specialist consultancy or introducing them to a training company for example, so where there is a much more deep intervention but not necessarily via the Business Link operating company itself. In other words, the Business Link operating company adviser will have introduced a third party into that client base."

Mr Martin Wyn Griffith, Chief Executive of the Small Business Service

House of Commons Trade and Industry, Minutes of Evidence 6 January, 2004

The Small Business Service classified SIBBP as "significant assistance", their most intense form of Business Link intervention. This activity went beyond the usual diagnostic process, i.e. "talking through with that business what their needs or opportunities might be."

Step 5 – Show Me The Money!

A key stimulus to the take up of SIBBP was the free money. The Department of Trade and Industry had committed to help fund resulting action plans proposed by Business Link Advisers. Each business could receive up to £5,000 to pay for consultant fees. However, this DTI Implementation Grant could only be accessed if a benchmark was submitted and the entire SIBBP process was complete. The second mandatory condition to qualify for funding was selection of consultant.

"This expert consultant will have a proven record of working with small businesses and will give you the advice and support you need to devise and run your project. In most cases, when a tailored project is recommended and undertaken, the DTI will also provide the funds for half of your project costs, up to a maximum of £5,000. You will provide the other half."

Achieving Best Practice in Your Business: An Introduction

Published by the Department of Trade and Industry - July 2004.

Cash would only be forthcoming if a small business chose to work with one of the "best practice experts" on the National Business Link Consultants Register. This database was an approved supplier list in all but name and caused a degree of disquiet in the consultancy sector.

Just by having a list meant a number of organisations were excluded, as not all consultants tried to qualify. Some did not even know about the existence of such a database, whilst others doubted the value of applying in the first place. The supplier list was a classic chicken and egg scenario. Advisers were reluctant to use the database, as there was a relatively small pool of consultants available, a proportion of which, they suspected, were in the lower quartile of performance because they needed Business Link to sell their product. This quality doubt may not have been based on fact, but it was real perception.

At the other end of the spectrum, it was questionable whether high quality consultancies would waste time and expense in preparing an application, knowing that Business Link was working with small and medium sized, often cash strapped businesses. Hard working consultants trying to make a living couldn't see the return on investment, as the potential for referrals appeared light. A number of good consultancies didn't trust Business Link advisers to pass on clients.

The Department of Trade and Industry had decided on the answer. The SIBBP scheme would remove adviser judgement altogether and make selection from the register a prerequisite to get the money. The Government was confident the accreditation process alone would guarantee best match. Despite the involvement of National Quality Assurance, this approval process appeared to be based primarily on holding the required level of public indemnity insurance and a portfolio of unconfirmed written references. More seriously, this model and future incarnations of supplier lists (Supplier Matching Service, S3) all presupposed a Business Link adviser was an unnecessary part of the selection process and should not exercise judgement.

By January 2005, over 800 SIBBP projects had been approved for funding. If each project received full entitlement, this is equivalent to a £4 million injection of tax-funded grant support put straight in the pockets of private sector consultants.

Step 6 – Shoulder Support

"While conducting the benchmarking exercise is useful, the real benefit will only be achieved if clear action plans and follow up result from that exercise. Organisations that participate in such benchmarking exercises could benefit from further support on what to do next, how to do it, and by when!"

Closing the Gap 3 (DTI Business Link and Cranfield University)
Neely, A.; Szwejczewski, M.; Jarrar, Y. - 20th September, 2002

Bringing in outsiders is a big step for any small business and a number start from a position of distrust and suspicion. The Business Link advisers helped prepare businesses to engage external consultancy, being willing to act as a devil on the shoulder, on hand to answer any questions and ensure all progressed as planned. The Personal Business Adviser transferred their personal knowledge and experience of what to expect and how to manage a consultancy project. This handholding exercise injected more confidence in the business owner and should have helped increase take up of external advice.

The follow up activity was deemed to be so critical to converting recommendation into action that it was designed into the process. SIBBP guidance stipulated a follow up meeting must take place, a minimum of six to twelve months, after an initial project had been started. At this point a business would be re-benchmarked to establish progress against all the baseline measures, highlighting any new weaknesses and strengths. Whether businesses and advisers had the time to repeat the process was debatable.

There would be no grant second time round.

Less is More

"The results from Wave 5 of the DTI Business Support Product Survey (2005) provide some corollary evidence on this point. Business Performance Diagnostic (SIBBP) recorded a lower score across a number of output measures than in the previous surveys. This would appear to be a result of the decline in overall satisfaction with the 'product'. One possible interpretation is that the respondent is more inclined to value the 'end result' (e.g. a grant application) of the diagnostic process rather than the process itself."

Economic Impact Study of Business Link Local Service - Project Report

Department for Business Enterprise and Regulatory Reform (BERR)

Saal, D; Mole, K; Roper, S and Hart, M (2006)

When grant support was removed from the SIBBP product, usage of the tool within the Business Links adviser team fell dramatically. It was not necessarily the product that was poor quality, rather that the value added to a business was uncertain.

Benchmarking is a broad map rather than a direct route to competitiveness. The pool of data on competitors was relatively small and each company was different in structure and size. Regional differences also played a part. In these circumstances what value can really be realised for a small business? Yes, the concept of managing key performance indicators could be communicated and results may well alert the organisation to weaknesses and strengths. However, any business adviser worth their salt would have achieved the same outputs without a 30 pages colour report.

In addition, the majority of small businesses just didn't have sophisticated enough systems in place to economically collect, monitor and evaluate this scale of data. Some small businesses don't know their gross profit margin, yet alone "value of supplies which are sub-standard on delivery" (question 53!). For larger organisations where information overload can be debilitating, there is no doubt benchmarking is a useful tool. However, the vast majority of SIBBP customers employed less than 20 persons, so much so that Winning Moves formally challenged the number of micro businesses being put through the process. Their revised policy stated categorically that value would be diluted for businesses employing less than 10 persons.

What cannot be disputed are the millions of pounds of grant money given to small businesses. This funding was intended to help businesses try and improve their performance using external consultancy. This stimulus was firmly in line with the original ethos of Business Link, to improve the take up of external knowledge. On that criteria alone SIBBP must be classified an expensive success.

In 2008 / 2009, the Department for Business, Enterprise and Regulatory Reform (BERR) executed a "timely exit from the Support to Implement Best Practice scheme." Their Annual Report and Accounts confirmed an annual value saving of £9.6 million. Since the launch in 2004, the Access and Support to Implement Best Practice Products had cost the Government a total of £44 million.[57]

Keeping Some Balance

After grant funding was withdrawn, the sudden drop off in SIBBP usage suggested the intended value had not been fully realised in the market place. The key weakness was not the process itself, which is still available today, albeit on a paid basis through the original designer Winning Moves (now claiming a benchmark bank of 100,000 data sets). Rather, that the product appeared focused on a comprehensive list of outcome measures, not drivers of performance.

A comparison with the earlier 1992 Balanced Scorecard system should be drawn. The two initiatives share common terminology. In Balanced Scorecard, a business focuses on measuring four core "perspectives" of the business – Financial, Customer, Internal Business Process, Learning and Growth. In the Benchmark Index, the questions were organised under headings using the same label of "perspectives" – Financial, Customer, People and Suppliers. Both products were based on the concept of "if you can't measure it, you can't manage it." However, there was one fundamental difference in their interpretation of this philosophy.

"Businesses are incredulous that a Balanced Scorecard of no more than two dozen measures can be sufficient for measuring their operations. They are, of course, correct in a narrow sense, but they fail to distinguish between diagnostic measures - those measures that monitor whether the business remains in control and can signal when unusual events are occurring that require immediate attention - and strategic measures - those that define a strategy designed for competitive excellence."

Translating Strategy into Action: The Balanced Scorecard
Robert S. Kaplan and David P. Norton (1996)

Kaplan and Norton believed monitoring a small number of performance drivers (measures) was more important to help a business grow than keeping your eye on a long list of outputs. Monitoring outputs is important to discover in a timely fashion whether something is going wrong, enabling remedial action. However, these measures should be "managed by exception" rather than key to strategic decision-making.

Far from limiting the number of questions, Winning Moves actually developed four more modules to add onto the core questionnaire - People and Skills (29 more measures), Business Processes (63 measures), Business Relationships – customers and suppliers (21 measures) and High performance Workplaces (34 measures).

Small businesses are time poor at the best of times and a lot of development activity will pivot around the owner or manager, who is using sight of the situation to manage the organisation. Whilst far from scientific, maybe educated "hunch and intuition" are acceptable, if not ideal, in a resource and time poor environment.

Kaplan and Norton used the human body analogy to reinforce the need to focus efforts on a small, but manageable, number of critical performance drivers.

"Many aspects of our bodily functions must perform within fairly narrow operating parameters if we are to survive. If our body temperature departs from a normal 1 - 2 degree window, or our blood pressure drops too low or escalates too high, we have a serious problem. In such circumstances, all our energies (and those of skilled professionals) are mobilized to restore these parameters to their normal levels. But we don't devote enormous energy to optimising our body temperature and blood pressure. Being able to control our body temperature to within 0.01 of the optimum will not be one of the strategic success factors that will determine whether we become a chief executive of a company, a senior partner in an international consulting firm, or a tenured full professor at a major university. Other factors are more decisive in determining whether we achieve our unique personal and professional objectives. Are body temperature and blood pressure important? Absolutely. Should these measurements fall outside certain control limits, we have a signal about a major problem that we must attend to and solve immediately. But while such measurements are necessary, they are not sufficient for the achievement of our long-run goals... Even the best objectives and measures can be achieved in bad ways."

Translating Strategy into Action: The Balanced Scorecard
Robert S. Kaplan and David P. Norton (1996)

In a small business environment, spending a lot of time implementing comprehensive systems to collect quantities of performance data may have seemed a tad over cooked, and not necessarily a good use of resource.

As US General George S. Patton (1885 – 1945) infamously said:

"A good plan, violently executed now, is better than a perfect plan next week."

CHAPTER NINE

HELP YOURSELF

"I am fully aware that the web and electronic data transmission has taken a quantum leap since I was involved in this field, so a lot of the information services could now be delivered through centralised one stop web shops that we didn't understand in the 90s. It's important that people like me don't immediately say just because I invented something in the 90s it's automatically right twenty years later. The concept is right. But the concept may not need such emphasis on physical one-stop shops."

The Rt Hon the Lord Heseltine CH

Interview with author at Haymarket Head Office, Hammersmith - 8th June, 2011

In a labour intensive organisation, the biggest cost is almost always payroll. Whatever the value of their work, the Business Link advisers didn't come cheap. Mark Prisk MP, Minister of State for Business and Enterprise, confirmed the cost of training and employing field-based Business Link advisers was £55.95 million in 2009 / 2010.[58] This estimate excluded expenses and overheads. Consequently, advisers were always in the spotlight, as government sought to sweat Business Links' most expensive asset.

In 1993, there was little choice but to rely on people to get out there and help businesses face to face. New technologies, such as the Internet and email, were in their infancy and still not widely available. As e-communication became more accessible the Government understandably looked at more efficient ways to mechanise the delivery of information and advice, reaching out to larger numbers of customers and reducing the reliance on human beings. Why have a small battalion of business advisers, with troublesome traits such as emotion and personal opinion, when a process driven solution might do the job in a consistent and methodical way?

To the left of the political spectrum it was hardly fair that a small number of elite businesses should receive the tax funded help. In the interest of equality everyone should get a piece of the pie.

"What I think is important is that the Business Link network is willing to work with anyone who wants to ask us for support."

David Irwin, CEO of the Small Business Service

House of Commons, Trade and Industry Minutes of Evidence 2nd May, 2001

As early as 2001, David Irwin, Chief Executive of the Small Business Service, confirmed his organisation had been given "a fairly major objective to target ALL micro businesses."

The Labour Government had publicly hung their stall on market penetration as the true measure of success.

"Business Link Operators were used by around 606,000 customers in 2003–04, comprising 435,000 existing firms (representing a 40 percent growth in use by existing firms between 2002–03 and 2003–04) and 171,000 pre-start businesses. Expressed as a ratio of the Inter-Departmental Business Register of 1.8 million firms (the largest official count), this is a market penetration rate of 34 per cent."

Mr Nigel Griffiths MP, Parliamentary Under-Secretary at Department of Trade and Industry. House of Commons Trade and Industry, Written Answers 21 July, 2004

You don't need to be a mathematician to realise a team of 1,000 business advisers would be sweating pretty damn hard to serve 600,000 businesses. Based on logistics as much as anything else, a drive for automation began.

Computer Says...

The Small Business Service launched the first ever Business Link call centre in April 2001. This centralised call handling facility was intended to increase engagement with small and medium sized businesses, enabling a team of telephone-based people to answer the more simple queries.

"The aim of the call centre and the web service is, on the whole, to give basic information, to be part of our overall promotional activity and to encourage businesses to consider a one-to-one conversation with a Business Link adviser."

David Irwin, CEO of the Small Business Service
House of Commons, Trade and Industry Minutes of Evidence 2nd May, 2001

This filtering was designed to push more customers through the Business Link funnel and ensure intensive assistance only went to those with highest potential. Despite appearances, expensive face-to-face advice was still not open to everyone. Advisers were only meant to work with higher growth entrepreneurs.

<u>First Contact</u>

The new Business Link Inquiry Service was based in Dundee and managed by British Telecom. From April 1st, 2001, all calls to the 0845 6009006 national number were routed to this central point, rather than direct to the respective Business Link in each region.

"We think it is very important we have enquiry handlers who can start with the client and where the client is at, rather than having a check list of questions and having to start at number one on the list, which has been my experience of call centres. We want the enquiry handler to be able to go straight to question nine if that is the right place."

David Irwin, CEO of the Small Business Service
House of Commons, Trade and Industry Minutes of Evidence 2nd May, 2001

The enquiry officers at the end of the phone would need a working knowledge of the issues facing businesses rather than being simple call handlers. David Irwin confirmed that all personnel were engaged in a "fairly major training programme" and that these people would not be "any old call centre enquiry handler who has nothing to do coming to work for us."

"If you asked for information about the Disability Discrimination Act, then, yes, the call centre will give you information about that. If you say, I would like a grant to start a dot-com business, then the person at the call centre will get a bit more information from you about what it is you really need, because my personal experience has been that most clients walk in and ask about a grant and as you talk to them you discover they have other issues."

David Irwin, CEO of the Small Business Service
House of Commons, Trade and Industry Minutes of Evidence 2nd May, 2001

150

To complement this formal training, the Small Business Service was keen that "a number of our own Business Link advisers come and spend some time in the call centre so they can hear some of the enquiries which are coming through, to give some immediate advice but also to help us identify the sort of extra training which may be required for these people."

The Business Link Enquiry Service was a risky venture, acknowledged even by the Labour Government's own backbench.

"Your reputation will go down very rapidly... if it does not work."

Helen Southworth MP - House of Commons Select Committees on Trade and Industry
House of Commons, Trade and Industry Minutes of Evidence 2nd May, 2001

Wrong Number?

On 22nd July, 2002, Nigel Griffiths MP confirmed that the Business Link Inquiry Service was part of the overall DTI Gateway (including a website and client database), which cost £2.65 million to set up and incurred annual expenditure of £3.75 million. He added that the "cost of the Business Link National Contact Centre cannot be disaggregated." In the first year of operation the number of telephone enquiries averaged 4,860 per month.[59] Whatever the final investment, the Small Business Service closed the National Contact Centre after just one year.

"The SBS has now concluded that instead of being handled by a centre service point, calls will be routed straight to local Business Link Operators. This will improve responsiveness and service to customers."

Mr Nigel Griffiths MP, Parliamentary Under-Secretary at DTI
House of Commons Hansard Written Answers for 8th March, 2002

Genius idea. Letting customers speak directly to their local advisers. Why had no one thought of that before... Business Links had been doing it this way for a decade prior to the SBS spending hundreds of thousands of taxpayer funds on an ill-fated call centre.

Online Time

A website for Business Link had been online since 1996. Produced by the Business Link Network Company, this site was hosted at Businesslink.co.uk and contained basic brochure content about the services available, including contact details for local partnerships. Like many early sites the Business Link website was decidedly uninspiring. Aside from moving the content about the screen and developing a few jazzy logo buttons, this web format remained relatively unchanged until 2001.

Website Hits

"I remind the House that 1.7 million small and medium sized enterprises are already IT-literate, and more than 450,000 of them have access to the web. The service that we now provide will continue to expand and evolve. A major objective of the web service is to provide personalised support enabling registered users to have their interests noted so that they can be automatically provided with up-to-date information and regulatory changes."

Mr Nigel Griffiths MP, Parliamentary Under-Secretary at DTI
House of Commons Debate held 13th July ,2001

The Small Business Service recognised that new technology was changing the way small and medium sized businesses were working. Their new portal hosted at Businesslink.Org created a site focused 100% on delivery of business information. Content guides included topics such as regulations and tax, finance and money, and starting a business.

On 19th September, 2002, Nigel Griffiths MP confirmed the www.businesslink.org website was being accessed 100,000 to 150,000 times each month, by over 30,000 businesses.[60]

152

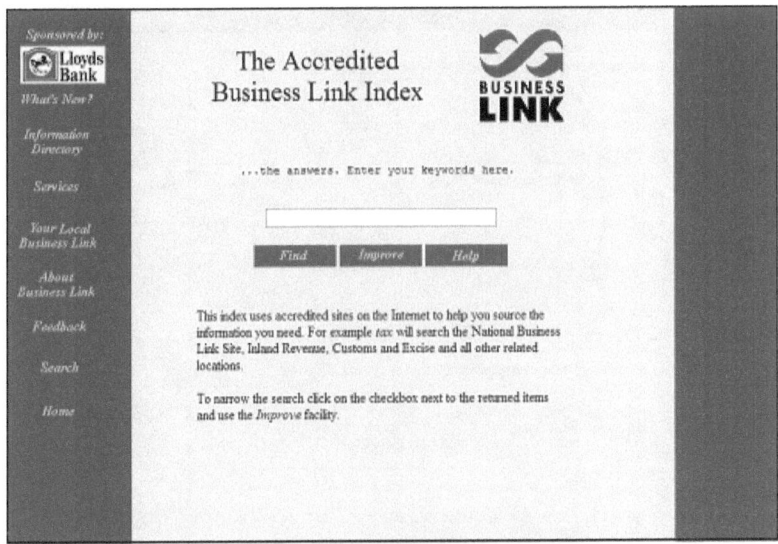

Screen grab from www.businesslink.co.uk - 19th December, 1996 [61]

This increase in performance was achieved on the back of sustained promotion. In October 2001, there was a national Business Link awareness campaign at a cost of £2.3 million. This activity was followed up by national newspaper and online advertising campaign in February 2002, costing a further £0.6 million. Nigel Griffiths MP reported that this investment stimulated a "55 percent increase in calls to the contact centre and a 96 percent increase in user sessions on the website." Despite this level of traffic, the website generated just 356 email enquiries to Business Link per month, a single email for every 421 visits.[62] The 2002 website was either exceptionally good at giving people the answers or visitors were being deterred from emailing. The homepage at that time listed a national Business Link telephone number, but no first page option to ask a question electronically. That might explain a lot.

Regardless of the number of enquiries, the traffic alone suggested businesses in the UK were hungry for online delivery of information.

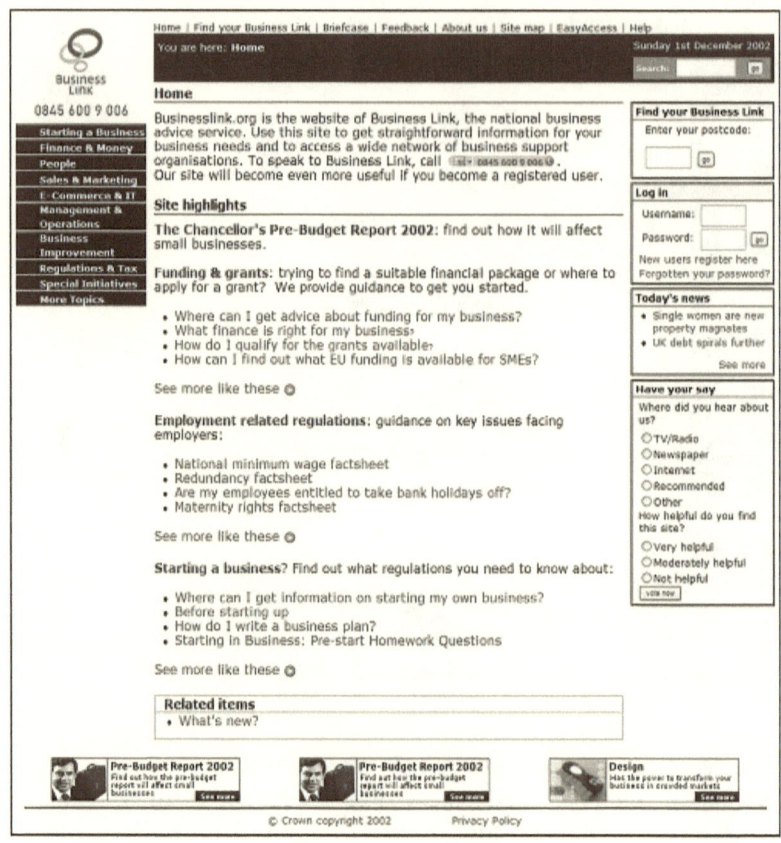

Screen grab from www.businesslink.org - 21st September, 2002 [63]

Business Link.gov.uk

In May 2004, the Small Business Service launched Business Link.gov.uk. Prior to this national website, each Business Link Operator retained the freedom to develop their own regional presence (with tailored content). Many of them did exactly that. However, each Business Link was now informed that independent websites were banned and there would be a single Business Link website for the country. Regional sites could be hosted at Business Link.gov.uk, but the core content would be the same, regardless of location.

"The site joins up national e-government services for the UK's small and medium-sized businesses, providing easy access to government regulatory and business support information, and to skills and training support. Usage of the site has exceeded targets since its launch. It is currently handling more than 400,000 user sessions each month."

Mr Nigel Griffiths MP, Parliamentary Under-Secretary at Department of Trade and Industry. House of Commons Hansard Written Answers for 20th October, 2004

The reaction from small and medium sized businesses was immediate. In the year ending March 2007, just three years after launch, it was announced that the number of unique visitors had exploded to 7 million users per annum.[64]

Technical evolution wasn't cheap. On 24th June, 2004, Patricia Hewitt, Minister for Small Business and E-Commerce, confirmed "the development of this major programme in 2003–04, including the former businesslink.org site, which it replaced in November 2004, cost £14.2 million."

Portal Combat

In December 2006, Sir David Varney published "Service transformation: A better service for citizens and businesses, a better deal for the taxpayer." This report, for the Chancellor of the Exchequer, was highly critical of "the number of departmental-specific websites'. David Varney was crystal clear on the solution: consolidate all of these independent sites into one single web portal – the Business Link national website.

"All departments will then have one corporate website utilizing shared infrastructure, and other websites will be closed."

Sir David Varney

Service transformation: A better service for citizens and businesses, a better deal for the taxpayer. December 2006

It was hoped that government would achieve efficiency savings by reducing the number of websites to be maintained and promoted. The Business Link national site would become the "primary information and transactional" channel for small and medium sized businesses. Migration of content commenced immediately.

On 31st March, 2008, the Public Accounts Committee published a review of progress on rationalisation and Varney's Transformation recommendations. The findings made pretty damning reading.

"After ten years of uncoordinated growth, the Government does not know exactly how many websites it operates, although it could be as many as 2,500. Over a quarter of government organisations still do not know the costs of their websites, making it impossible to assess whether they are value for money. 16% of government organisations have no data about how their websites are being used."

Government on the Internet: Progress in delivering information and services online: a review of progress on consolidation (16th report of session 2007 / 2008)

A new political urgency saw the Business Link.gov.uk website increase in size by 400 percent over the next two years.

By 31st March, 2010, a total of 1,001 of the 1,795 websites identified in the report had been shut down. 289 sites had been given approval to continue and 422 had been put forward for closure.[65] On 1st April, 2011, the "migration of content and transactions from over 170 government websites to the Business Link website was completed.[66]

The Government put in place a series of policy checks to prevent such fragmentation and information overload ever happening again.

"This Government is completely committed to getting the government web back under control. The days of 'vanity' sites are over. It is not good enough to have websites, which do not deliver the high quality services, which people expect and deserve. That is why we will take tough action to get rid of those which are not up to the job and do not offer good value for money and introduce strict guidelines for those that remain."

Francis Maude MP, Minister for the Cabinet Office
Coalition Government Cabinet Press Notice – 24th June, 2010

Supersize Shopping Cart

On 7th November, 2005, the management of the Business Link national website was outsourced to private sector service company Serco Group. Under the contract, Serco would be "responsible for developing and delivering the BusinessLink.gov programme."

"Part of the Small Business Service mission is to foster entrepreneurial cultures and help people achieve their potential. Serco shares these ambitions. We will draw on capability from across Serco to support their achievement through this contract (BL.gov)."

Christopher Hyman, Serco Group Chief Executive Officer
Serco Group Press Release – 7th November, 2005

The press release went onto confirm "the contract with the Department of Trade and Industry is due to start immediately. The service will run for five years with up to four additional one-year renewals, and could be valued at more than £125m over this extended period." This level of spending was only ever seriously questioned when the Central Office of Information (COI) published "Reporting on Progress: Central Government Websites 2009 / 2010." The research confirmed the Business Link.gov.uk service was costing £35 million per annum on non-staff costs alone. Expenditure included £6.2 million for strategy and planning, £4.3 million design and build, £4.6 million hosting and infrastructure, £15.2 million content provision and £4.4 million testing and evaluation. An additional

£788,000 funded 12 staff (Full Time Equivalents) working on the project.

In return, the taxpayer investment had created a business information and advice website generating 16,670,665 visits each year. These users accessed 93,502,545 pages of information during the period 2009 to 2010.[67] These sums were difficult to comprehend for some, but the raw data enabled the estimate of a "per visit" cost - an incendiary figure of £2.15.

On 7th July, 2010, the BBC Journalist Rory Cellan-Jones wrote that in terms of cost only the "NHS Choices site, at £21m, comes anywhere close. But it has around six million unique users a month, whereas the Business Link site, which offers all kinds of advice to businesses, has just over a million." In the same article Sean O'Halloran of Hoop Associates (public sector website consultancy) was quoted as saying "It's a completely unfathomable number, I can't imagine how that could be spent."

A feeding frenzy of criticism played out on all the major business forums.

Checking Out

What exactly does a £125 million website buy you?

The Business Link.gov.uk Annual Review for 2009 / 2010 confirmed that in less than two years the site had quadrupled in size. That's lot of content development and coding. Serco was also closing in on their three years target to migrate 95% of other business related government websites into Business Link.Gov.uk. This simplification was demanded by Sir David Varney's Transformation programme in 2006. No easy feat, logistically or politically.

During the same period, the campaign support service launched, creating "channel shift savings" for 10 different government departments, or in less technical speak, cost savings using a central

158

marketing resource. The 31 campaigns run through Business Link.gov.uk attracted over 2.9 million visitors.[68]

The national site was a ruthless converter with over 31% of visitors choosing to make a transaction i.e. using an information tool on the site. This conversion rate is virtually unheard of in the private sector. This feat can only be linked to effective usability, quality of content and targeted online marketing (the conversion rate was over 50 percent for pay per click traffic).

The investment looked shaky when the cost per visitor was evaluated in isolation. However, Business Link.gov.uk was at core an information and advice portal, not a commodity seller. The true return on investment should be measured by how many people used the website information to make money and employ more people, not the number of downloads and click count. The 2010 Her Majesty's Revenue and Customs (HMRC) Annual Review for Business Link.gov claimed users of the website achieved combined savings of £296 million over a 12 months period and performance improvements worth over £500 million. A separate Serco commissioned report the previous year claimed "more than £1 billion of savings and benefits." In 2010, the Business Link national website achieved a customer satisfaction rating of 93 percent.

Not for the first time, the subjective views of customers themselves seemed to take second fiddle to statistics as these figures were hardly mentioned by critics. During the same 12 months of strongest criticism, over 1.18 million users accessed the "calculate your employees holiday entitlement" tool. Over 91,000 downloaded "International Trade – The Basics." A total of 261,974 people read "Prepare a Business Plan" and 701,946 searched the grants database. A total of 2,409 people even went as far to download "Sheep and Goats identification, registration and movement" - that much lesser known route to competitive advantage!

The £125 million investment was delivering business advice and information to the masses for the first time in history. Media coverage of this achievement was a ripple at best. Most were quick to judge, taking little account of the asset value of the growing content.

On 17th February, 2011, the National Audit Office (NAO) published "Delivering Regulatory Reform." Their survey, of 12,000 businesses, claimed only 34 actually used the Business Link website. The report went on to claim over a quarter of small businesses "are not online and so would not have access to web-based information." The research concluded the majority of entrepreneurs use "trade associations and experts" as their main source of support, not Business Link. In stark contrast, the HMRC Annual Report on BusinessLink.gov.uk for 2010 reported over 19.4 million visits to the website (audited figures). Over 5.7 million online diagnostics had been completed by businesses in that financial year and 100,000 users registered their personal details on the website.

The two performance appraisals didn't quite correlate. Whatever the reality, yet again a bad news message was circulated in the business press. Regardless, the Government remained firmly committed to websites as the future of business support in this country.

Electric Dreams

"Our thinking in this area is that we must make the service more personalised, more widely known and more focused on business customers 'self-serving' – not just with simple information queries, but with at least some elements of self diagnosis when their business has a challenge or a difficulty."

Business Link.gov.uk Annual Review 2009-2010

Published By Her Majesty's Revenue and Customs 27th July, 2010

The Businesslink.Org website set the foundation for the delivery of online business support right up to present day. The different section headings agreed in 2003 still formed the content structure used on the site in 2011. Businesses could now access a vast amount of expert data and complete many of the transactions needed to run an organisation in the UK. The simple brochure site, from the nineties, had evolved into a monster bank of business data and a "single, online government service for businesses of all sizes." Lord Heseltine's "one stop web shop" in any other name.

Screen grab from www.businesslink.gov.uk - 23rd August, 2011 [69]

The vision for automated advice to the masses had been realised, albeit at a fairly significant cost to the taxpayer. On 31st March, 2011, all the regional pages on Business Link.gov.uk were finally closed. Any relevant content was migrated to the main website. Face to face advisory services would be pulled later that year on 25th November, being replaced by an improved "self-serving" Business Link.gov.uk website and a shiny brand new National Contact Centre.

Sound familiar? Was this a case of history repeating itself or the inevitable march of technological progress? Whatever the reality, the anti-intervention lobby was adamant; small businesses are more than capable of sorting out their own problems. Besides, it's cheaper that way too. If you were a small business, the message was clear.

Go and help yourself.

CHAPTER TEN

LOCALISM

2005

"Given that the Regional Development Agencies (RDA) are responsible for the economic development of their regions, they will inevitably have to work closely with, and have regard to the views of, business in their areas. If, as one business organisation told us, businesses do not 'actually know what they want', the RDAs can hardly be expected to deliver support effectively."

House of Commons Select Committee on Trade and Industry
Fifth Report
9th June, 2004

In 1999, the Labour Government established eight Regional Development Agencies for the West Midlands, East of England, East Midlands, Northwest, North East, South East, South West and Yorkshire (and Humberside). The London Development Agency would follow a year later. These new government funded bodies had responsibilities under the Regional Development Agencies Act 1998 to develop their own local economies:

- Furthering economic development and regeneration;

- Promoting business efficiency, investment and competitiveness;

- Promoting employment;

- Enhancing the development of skills relevant to employment

- Contributing to sustainable development.

For small and medium sized businesses, these enigma organisations would remain just that, with only the smallest fraction receiving direct help.

Different Strokes for Different Folks

The birth of these new Agencies came about at the height of Tony Blair's Regional agenda. Power was being devolved away from Central Government and put back in the hands of local people. This quiet revolution stripped authority away from Civil Servants in London and transferred responsibility for economic strategy to the Provinces.

Each Agency was tasked with creating a Regional Economic Strategy for their respective areas. These plans were not based purely on economics, but also took into account the social development of the region, including a Tier 1 objective to "promote social cohesion and sustainable development through integrated local regeneration programmes." In layman's language, improve the lifestyle of your population in the long term by simplifying support. This new order was under immediate attack from both top and bottom.

Clinging to Power

"When RDAs were established they were required to publish a Regional Economic Strategy, setting out their goals for their regions and broadly speaking, the means by which these goals might be achieved. However, with funds allocated through pre-committed funding streams, there was little scope for progress towards implementing these strategies."

House of Commons Trade and Industry Committee

Support to Businesses from Regional Development Agencies

Fifth Report of Session 2003–04 – 11th May, 2004

On paper, government policy had devolved power, but in reality the Department of Trade and Industry and others linked funding to the achievement of a glut of targets. This preserved their influence as Departments sought to drive their own schemes and agendas.

The Regional Development Agencies were being coerced into implementing the plans of other organisations, propping up complexity rather than implementing simplification. This conditional funding tied the hands of the RDA and reduced their ability to make autonomous decisions on their future.

Single Pot

In April 2002, the Government decided the only way to overcome the situation was to pool all the funding into a single pot of cash. Each Department would no longer be able to insist on how their respective investments were managed. Money would now be allocated to each RDA as a no strings lump sum. The Agencies would thus hold sufficient independence to act in the best interest of their businesses. The Department of Trade and Industry would continue to govern the RDA but would have no influence on how their funds were committed.

In the public sector nothing comes without strings and RDA budgets would still be dependent on hitting a number of headline targets. However, the regions now had just one taskmaster, a step forward in anyone's book.

The single pot was not insignificant. In 2003, the RDAs were allocated £1.7 billion of taxpayer funding.

Brains not Brawn

The RDA had a strategic role and only the largest threats and opportunities would encourage them to get their hands dirty.

John Burrow, Director of Business Development for the Northwest Development Agency (NWDA) explained "more direct, face-to-face contact between the RDA and an individual company is likely to arise only where that company has a large enough presence to be classed as regionally strategic." There were 180,000 businesses in the North West at the time. "In the case of the North West this definition encompasses some 400 companies."[70] This figure was 0.2% of businesses in the area.

In this context, it is hardly surprising so many businesses complained the RDA never did anything for them. The perception was you could only gain the attention of the RDA if you threatened to make a significant number of people redundant (less than fifty wouldn't cause a ripple), were looking to pump tens of millions into new businesses (new jobs) or plain threatened to make trouble in the press.

Businesses didn't understand the strategic remit and became increasingly disgruntled at the apparent lack of effort and direct help on the ground. Yet the RDA was never meant to engage at a micro level. The function of these organisations was primarily strategic, thinking long term and for the future. Most Regional Economic Strategies were 5 to 10 years in duration, an incomprehensible period to most small businesses, but a realistic timescale when looking to transform infrastructure, skills, economies and social development. The RDA relied on strategic partners (such as Business Link) to do the day-to-day dirty work and implement their plans.

Tanks on the Lawn

"We believe that RDAs can play a valuable role in developing their regional economies and helping businesses located there. However, in order to do so, they need the authority to implement their strategies. We are concerned that the institutional clutter at regional and sub-regional level is hindering this: too many vested interests are limiting the scope and effectiveness of action by the RDAs."

House of Commons Trade and Industry Committee
Support to Businesses from Regional Development Agencies
Fifth Report of Session 2003–04 – 11th May, 2004

Business support had become an industry in itself and like anyone else in the private sector the primary objective was survival. Existing suppliers greeted the imposition of the RDA with a degree of suspicion. And their concerns were proven to be somewhat validated.

In 2004, Martin Wyn Griffith, CEO of the Small Business Service, believed the RDA was in the midst of a "massive consultation process within their region to get those players to understand that being a turkey voting for Christmas might actually be a reality here and that there will have to be some rationalisation." He went on to affirm that this would be survival of the fittest and that any providers not up to scratch would "disappear." This approach was hardly textbook how to win friends and influence people.

The RDA was short of allies and when their demise finally came there would be no queue of willing supporters ready to defend them.

Quango Conflict

For Business Link the RDA came to the fore when the Small Business Service was established in 2001. The visions for these two bodies sounded suspiciously similar.

"Our key objectives are to further economic development, promote business efficiency, innovation and training, promote employment opportunities, contribute to the achievement of sustainable development and improve the quality of life for everyone (in the region).

East of England Development Agency Website - www.eeda.org.uk
5th April, 2001

"Our purpose is to help build an enterprise society in which small businesses can thrive and achieve their potential. We will do this by developing and maintaining a world class business support service to enhance their competitiveness and profitability, championing entrepreneurship across society and particularly in under-represented and disadvantaged groups."

Small Business Service Website - www.sbs.gov.uk
28th April, 2001

In 2001, David Irwin, Chief Executive Officer of the Small Business Service, was nonplussed and believed everyone still had a part to play. The RDA would create a regional strategy, the SBS would manage Business Links to help implement that plan, and the individual franchisees would get stuck in on the ground

"The RDA have a role to ensure everyone is coming together, everyone is happy with the strategy but also that the strategy is right for the region."

David Irwin, CEO of the Small Business Service
Select Committee on Trade and Industry Minutes of Evidence - 2nd May, 2001

Four years on and Irwin's successor would put a very different spin on events.

"Before my time there I think the relationship was characterised as fairly adversarial, there was really quite a sense of 'what do you need the Small Business Service (SBS) for, the RDAs can do this' from the RDA camp, and the SBS was looking at the RDAs as a group of organisations that were attempting to take over their turf and it was all about 'tanks on the lawn' and all that."

Mr Martin Wyn Griffith, CEO of the Small Business Service
House of Commons Trade and Industry Minutes of Evidence, 6th January, 2004

Whatever the true relationship behind closed doors, small and medium sized businesses remained largely unaware of any conflict (or the organisations themselves for that matter).

Missing Link

"The RDAs are pretty clear that the SBS has a role to play at a national level in terms of influencing other government departments. We also have a role to play in the regions working alongside the RDAs to make sure that business support is rationalised effectively in each region and that the RDAs' role is to take the lead in doing that. If managing Business Link Operators on our behalf through a contracted chain is part of that equation then that is absolutely fine."

Mr Martin Wyn Griffith, CEO of the Small Business Service
House of Commons Trade and Industry Minutes of Evidence, 6th January, 2004

If the Government really wanted to create power for the people in the regions, why would the largest business support network in history still be managed from London? It didn't take long for people to start asking why the RDA didn't have the Business Links.

<u>Provincial Pilots</u>

The Government had hoped regional control would lead to a more targeted deployment of the Business Link resource, local solutions to local problems.

In 2002, the Government launched three pilot projects to explore how RDAs could lead a Business Link service. These trials were conducted in the North West, East Midlands and West Midlands. Each RDA was given the freedom to create their own business model, resulting in three very different approaches.

The North West joined with the SBS and focused on developing a set suite of products for small businesses, reducing duplication of services and engaging the wider business support network. For Business Links, this meant a more formal separation of brokerage and delivery, in effect the hands off notice and lighter role. Significantly, the North West RDA committed to "institutional streamlining" and merging Business Links in their area.

In the East Midlands the RDA chose to take over exclusive responsibility for Business Links in their area. The SBS were surplus to requirements.

West Midlands was different again, deciding to focus on sector development. Their single pot was used to ramp up this activity through Business Link and "a much looser management arrangement" was agreed with the SBS.[71]

Despite these differences, a common drive in the pilots was simplification of business support, particularly any contractual arrangements. The Small Business Service management of Business Links suddenly seemed a trifle over cooked.

"You have got the concept that SBS manages a contract with the RDA to manage a contract with the Business Link Operator on the ground: so rather than a national organisation contracting directly with a local organisation, we contract with the region and allow the region the flexibility to determine how it plays sub-regionally."

Mr Martin Wyn Griffith, Chief Executive Small Business Service

House of Commons Trade and Industry Minutes of Evidence, 6th January, 2004

Effectively, the taxpayer was paying a supervisor to supervise a supervisor. A second round of Business Link rationalisation was on the cards.

Under New Management

The Government was more than satisfied with the results of the pilots. Nine regional partnerships would be easier to manage than 45 independent Business Link organisations. Decision-making could be moved out of London to the provinces, closer to small businesses. Then the RDA alone could decide how best to spend their pots of cash, the hope being that businesses would ask for different support, rather than being told what they needed.

Gordon Brown MP, the Chancellor of the Exchequer, announced in his 2004 Budget speech, that full control of the Business Links would pass to all the Regions in April 2005.

"We want the Small Business Service to concentrate on those areas of policy that affect small business. That is what its core responsibilities are. I think the RDAs are far better placed to provide frontline services... I took the view not just that we need to simplify the number of things that we offer people; I would also like to reduce the number of places that you get them."

Alistair Darling MP, Secretary of State for Trade and Industry

House of Commons: Trade and Industry Minutes of Evidence 24th October, 2006

Business Link would remain the preferred brand for business support. However, the RDA would follow through on their early intentions and slash the number of Business Link contracts from 45 to just 15.

As in 2001, the existing Business Link Operators had first opportunity to bid uncontested for the new contracts. Competitive tender would only kick in if the organisations could not agree to collaborate (effectively merge). In most regions an amicable settlement was reached, but not always. In the South West, Business Link Somerset and Business Link Devon and Cornwall would undertake a fairly acrimonious consultation, resulting in failure to present a joint proposal. This opened the tender to external bidders. The contract was finally awarded to a Serco / Somerset Business Link bid, but not without first incurring a fair degree of pain and press criticism. Politics and self-interest remained ever present in the business support sector and this friction was not confined just to Business Links.

"Achieving partner buy-in has taken longer than anticipated. The clear message emerging from the assessment is therefore that while the regions are potentially best placed strategically to manage local delivery of business support, the RDAs will need time and support to develop their capacity and capability to deliver."

Select Committee for the Treasury

Fourth Special Report, Session 2003 / 2004

Time was not a luxury afforded to the RDA. The Business Link network had been slashed from 80 independent operators to 15 organisations in less than six years. In less time than that, the Regional Development Agencies would be consigned to history.

Active Agent

Regional Development Agencies controlled over £1.5 billion of taxpayer funding per annum. In January 2010, the report "RDA Delivering for Communities" announced the results of an independent review by PriceWaterhouseCoopers. This report declared that every £1 invested by RDAs to date had generated £4.50 in return.

The evidence suggested the Regional Development Agencies were making a difference to businesses and communities.

Yet within Business Links and the wider business community the Regional Development Agencies were frequently criticised for being out of touch with the needs of small businesses, particularly within the adviser teams themselves. This perception was driven by the RDA's apparent stance that bums on seats was the mark of success rather than really helping businesses, a view simplistic in the extreme, but not entirely without foundation.

"Although the budgets have not gone up, the performance of the Business Links certainly has. We are trying to see *more* businesses than ever before."

Jim Braithwaite – Chairman, South East England Development Agency

House of Commons Minutes of Evidence SEEDA 11th May, 2009

Why was there such a disjoint between actual achievement and perceived failure? What exactly did the RDA do for small and medium sized businesses?

Cluster Bomb

Each Regional Development Agency created a tailored economic strategy for their respective areas. These documents were meticulously researched by the RDA and formed a detailed business plan for the next five to ten years. A common element in all regional economic strategies was an enthusiasm for cluster thinking, the aspect of most relevance to a small business. Each RDA had identified a handful of sectors that were critical to making their areas more competitive. Advanced engineering and creative industries were pretty much common to all, although that didn't mean the strategies followed a template. For example, the East of England Development Agency highlighted oil and gas in Great Yarmouth, not something likely to be of great strategic importance in Penzance.

The RDA, supported by the Small Business Service, now demanded Business Links nurture and encourage these key industries by including sector specific targets within their own business plans.

The concept was fairly simple. Identify a concentration of businesses in a region that share related activities, suppliers and institutions. Encourage these organisations to communicate, collaborate and work more closely together. The sum of the parts would be greater than the one, sharing best practice and achieving economies of scale.

Cluster thinking can be spectacular when it works, technology in Cambridgeshire being one such example. In reality this is a lot harder than it sounds, requiring dedicated resource and investment to set up networks. Cluster strategies only work with careful segmentation of the market and a targeted deployment of your resources. It is no place for a Business Link broad brush.

For example, in Business Link Norfolk they satisfied the RDA demand for immediate action by labelling each existing adviser a "sector specialist." This approach had varying degrees of success depending on each adviser's day-to-day commitments and their enthusiasm for the sector. In essence it was a one person and his dog deal, without the dog. Even with a degree of lip service, labels did at least focus activity on certain sectors, albeit at the expense of other industries less deserving in the eyes of the RDA.

Performance Engineer

"We took over the Business Link service two years ago, reducing five Business Links to one, which has allowed us to increase the number of frontline advisers by 40% and reduce back office costs by over a third."

Paddy Tipping, Chairman of the East Midlands Development Agency

House of Commons East Midlands Regional Committee Minutes of Evidence

27th April, 2009

Regional Development Agencies revolutionised the way Business Links supported small and medium sized businesses. The RDA slashed the number of Business Link Operators by two thirds and claimed this new "streamlined regional delivery" model resulted in lower overhead, as a single back office function now sufficed within each region.

"Over the past three years, these costs have come down from 31% of the total annual funding to 23% per annum with plans to reduce these even further. These efficiency gains are being reinvested in front line delivery resulting in improved performance."

Business and Enterprise Committee - Written Evidence Session 2008 2009

Regional development agencies and the Local Democracy, Economic Development and Construction Bill

Prepared 13th March, 2009.

What was in no doubt at all was more upheaval to the service and a constant demand for increasing volume. The targets for each Personal Business Adviser doubled, sometimes trebled, during the reign of the RDA. The Business Links were evolving into production operations, moving further away from creative knowledge transfer. The Personal Business Advisers remained fully committed to helping small businesses but now had half the time for each client and were commanded to signpost rather than advise. A move guaranteed to have an impact on any frontline service.

More worryingly for small businesses the rationalisation of Business Links caused a fairly dramatic culture shift. Intensive assistance used to be evidenced by client comments, customer satisfaction and financial impact. In the performance management culture created by the RDA, the emphasis shifted significantly towards a signed action plan and financial forecast, essentially ticking two boxes.

The demand for volume engagement inevitably drove adviser behaviour. Target language evolved. Advisers were now being asked to "I.A." faceless customers (obtain signed paperwork and add to database). Real life detail was in danger of becoming superfluous.

This approach sat uncomfortably with many advisers, who felt this devalued the service and was not in line with the original vision.

Business Links needed knowledge and experience to deliver for the RDA, but now they also needed a flair for administration, rare traits in any business consultant. Paper work is not a big chapter in the 'advisory handbook'. The mandatory requirement to have experience running your own business had been removed from job descriptions and adverts. Within three years in the South West, over 10 years had been sliced off the average age of an adviser, welcomed by some who believed a less mature team would be more dynamic and able to connect more readily with customers.

Regardless, and to their credit, the fifteen new Business Links reengineered operations to meet the latest demand of more for less.

"Since RDAs took over the responsibility for the management of the Business Link (BL) network the number of customers using BL service has increased by 29% to over 856,000 customers and those receiving in-depth support has increased by 73% to over 65,000 businesses. At the same time customer satisfaction results have remained consistently high at around 90%."

Business and Enterprise Committee - Written Evidence Session 2008 2009

Regional development agencies and the Local Democracy, Economic Development and Construction Bill

Prepared 13th March, 2009.

The RDAs had undoubtedly achieved what they set out to do, increasing the number of businesses in their area receiving advice and support. However, during the same period Personal Business Advisers were typically targeted to work with 100% more customers, effectively halving the time available for each business. If you were a small business, you were still being helped, just a little less so.

Market penetration was no defense against a potent mix of customer complaint (however insignificant statistically) and research reports that questioned the impact of the Business Link service. When the

176

end came, spreading the jam thinly to reach the masses was a nail in the coffin for public funded advisory services.

Shred Tape

One achievement not in dispute was the RDA campaign to simplify how businesses access support.

"We have massively simplified business support in the region as part of national policy (Business Support Simplification Programme) and gone from some 3,000 products nationally to 30 and fewer."

Paddy Tipping, Chairman of the East Midlands Development Agency
House of Commons East Midlands Regional Committee Minutes of Evidence
27th April, 2009

The RDA leadership of the Business Support Simplification Programme (BSSP) ushered in the most radical change to business support in a decade.

CHAPTER ELEVEN

NO WRONG DOOR

2007 to 2010

"Many businesses say they are confused. Little coordination, numerous schemes and multiple providers mean that some companies, particularly time and cash strapped SMEs, are put off seeking help. The Annual Small Business Service Survey 2005 found that over 50% of small businesses want government help, but struggle to find their way through the maze of provision."

Simple Support, Better Business: Business Support in 2010
Department for Business, Enterprise and Regulatory Reform (BERR)
Published March 2008

The Business Support Simplification Programme (BSSP) was first announced in the 2006 Budget. Previous attempts at simplification had focused on using Personal Business Advisers as navigators to guide small businesses through the labyrinth of different business support schemes. It was the advisers' role to know what help was out there, so that small businesses didn't need to.

"For the first time ever, government departments have published rolling simplification programmes, outlining measures to reduce burdens for business. That is why we attach particular importance to better regulation and are committed to reducing the burden of regulation on business by 25 per cent, a total saving across government of £2 billion by 2010, with BERR playing its part, reducing its burden by about £700 million by 2010."

Mr Pat McFadden MP, Minister of State for Employment Relations and Postal Affairs,

Department for Business, Enterprise & Regulatory Reform (BERR)

Commons Debates. Written Answers to Questions – 18th October, 2007

The Business Support Simplification Programme (BSSP) approach to the maze of business support was more direct and uncompromising.

Why pay a guide when you can just chop down the hedges?

Collateral Damage

The Government planned to reduce their support schemes from 3,000 to 100 within four years.

The pre-budget report in 2007 announced that Business Link would remain the "primary access route" for businesses seeking support. Everything would now flow through Business Link whether small businesses or the business support sector liked it or not.

In the event, the Government forgot to put the brakes on. In their enthusiasm for BSSP the number of support schemes was slashed to just thirteen. Whilst no doubt simplifying the support landscape, the flipside was 2,987 initiatives effectively disappeared. Casualties were inevitable.

Managed Out

On 13th June, 2006, the Confederation of British Industry (CBI) pledged immediate support for the BSSP, whilst making the obligatory claim to have had the idea in the first place. However, they cited one minor reservation in their announcement.

"We therefore support the efforts by the Small Business Service (SBS) to cut the number to 100 (schemes) by 2010, but again question whether the SBS will have sufficient clout across Whitehall to deliver this initiative in a manner that will benefit businesses."

Letter from CBI to the Committee Chairman
House of Commons Public Accounts Minutes of Evidence Session 2006 2007
15th January, 2007.

Prior to BSSP, the Small Business Service had already managed their own rationalisation process, the most significant outcome of this project being the marked reduction in the number of Business Link operators. However, any credit for these achievements was somewhat rained on when the Government decided the SBS itself was part of the problem and added to the confusion. Consequently, in April 2007, the Government converted the Small Business Service into a policy directorate within the Department of Trade and Industry's Enterprise and Business Group. This act severed the organisation's direct links to business support. The SBS had supported simplification from the start. However, ultimately it was decided they themselves must give way to make "Business Link the principle focus."[72]

The Regional Development Agencies were the new champions for small business.

Managed In

"A vital part of the BSSP will be improvements to the Business Link service to provide a high quality, consistent service which growing businesses feel confident to use. Some Business Links have already begun to reform with good progress made. Ultimately, business should be able to access support at any point through a 'no wrong door' approach and be confident of being sign-posted correctly, regardless of the final provider of the service."

Memorandum Submitted by the CBI

House of Commons Business and Enterprise Committee

Written Evidence Session 2008 2009

The Business Link network now consisted of just fifteen organisations covering the entire country, under the direct control of the RDA. The next step for government would be to take on the advisers themselves.

Historically, Business Links had always used a number of different field teams, the generalist Personal Business Advisers, an international trade team, design and innovation, financial advice, online business and so on. Collaboration was highly dependent on personal relationships. As a result, the degree of help small businesses received was variable.

In the ideal world the generalist adviser would visit a small business, identify where support was needed and refer in specialist colleagues to transfer the required knowledge. This approach would result in a business seeing up to five different advisers. As well as being time intensive for the small business itself, the powers that be deemed this approach to be costly and confusing.

The Government remained firmly committed to signposting, not in depth advice. The need for experts fell, as you no longer needed to know the answers, just the questions. This simplistic outlook neutralised a key advantage of using specialist teams. These people were dedicated to a single field of knowledge. Specialists had relationships with a smaller number of consultants, academics and customers in their sector. As a result, these relationships were more developed and specialists really were expert brokers. To a small business this meant a better 'match' and consequently better business solutions.

Regardless of the benefits, specialists faced extinction in the name of simplicity.

Super Brokers

"The aim is to establish a 'no wrong door' approach so employers know who to turn to for all of the help they need. The work of Business Link, local Learning and Skills Councils and Job Centre Plus will be aligned. It is particularly important that the generalist Business Link brokerage service is effectively integrated with the specialist Train to Gain skills brokers and there is a simple customer journey for employers."

Memorandum submitted by the Department of Trade & Industry

House of Commons Trade and Industry Minutes of Evidence

6th March, 2007

Train to Gain was the Government's £925 million per annum national skills service.[73] This organisation was tasked to "support employers of all sizes, in all sectors, to improve the skills of their employees as a route to improving their business performance." The Train to Gain skills brokers delivered an Integrated Brokerage Service through Business Link, which coordinated free and subsidised training, promoted National Vocational Qualifications (NVQ) and encouraged the take up of apprenticeships.

When the integration of specialist adviser teams was first muted, the Business Link field teams immediately assumed the Government were trying to create the 'super broker'. These accusations were rebutted repeatedly by management, which did little to allay suspicions that the adviser service was being dumbed down to save a buck. The mythical 'super broker' is an adviser who is omniscient about business. The creation of specialist advisers in the first place had come about precisely because it is impossible for one person to know everything about business, leading to a shallower diagnosis and missed opportunities.

On April 1st, 2009, the Department of Trade and Industry effectively closed the Train to Gain initiative. The scheme's skills specialists transferred into Business Link organisations and were retagged generalist advisers. Overnight, this integration increased the number of Personal Business Advisers working in Business Links from 854 to 1,021 persons, a 20 percent spike.[74]

The Government claimed immediate advantages for small businesses.

"The Department has introduced a range of measures to streamline Train to Gain for employers and skills providers and to simplify access. For example, we have brought together the Train to Gain and Business Link brokerage services to make it easier for businesses to identify the learning requirements of their staff, alongside their wider business needs."

Kevin Brennan MP. Minister of State for FE, Skills, Apprenticeships and Consumer Affairs. House of Commons Hansard Debates, Written Answers 21st October, 2009

At the coalface, this drive for a "comprehensive information, diagnostic and brokerage service" caused an instant skills gap.[75] The majority of skills advisers had not been trained in general business disciplines such as sales and marketing. They were expert in people issues but had minimal experience advising customers on general business. Similarly, the Personal Business Advisers had always been hand held by the Train to Gain team. When it came to training and people development, most did not have an in depth knowledge of the different initiatives and specialist providers of support.

Business Links were instantly challenged to get both sides up to speed and prevent the quality of service from falling. Predictably, the Regional Development Agencies intervened to demand consistency throughout this process, compelling Business Links to use the Small

Firms Training Enterprise Initiative (SFEDI) standards again. Skills advisers would complete the general SFEDI standard. Personal Business Advisers would complete a new SFEDI skills adviser module. The assessment process would take between six and twelve months to complete. In the South West the cost to complete each accreditation was £2,000 per adviser. If all 1,021 advisers completed SFEDI at this same rate the total cost was over £2 million.

Solutions for Business (SfB)

"The Government announced Solutions for Business, their streamlined portfolio of business support products, in October 2008, with 30 schemes to be in place by March 2009, all other schemes will have closed, or been given notice to close by March 2010. Business Link will be the main access channel to this support. The Government have committed to keep the streamlined portfolio at less than 100 products in total, covering all of the £2.5 billion spend on business support."

Ian Pearson MP, Economic Secretary to the Treasury
House of Commons Hansard Debates, Written Answers – 27th April, 2009

When the dust settled, the Government had retained a baker's dozen of products for small and medium sized businesses. In 2011, the thirteen survivors from the cull were:

1 - Collaborative Research and Development

Designed to assist the industrial and research communities to work together on R&D projects.

2 - Designing Demand

If you were a SME, with the potential for high growth, you could get up to 10 days of design and innovation focussed mentoring.

3 - Finance for Business

Loans offered up to £250,000 and equity investment up to £2 million (two-thirds public supplemented by one third private).

4 - Grant for Research and Development

Grants to help carry out research and development on innovative technological products / services (35% and 60% of project value).

5 - Helping Your Business Grow Internationally

Prepare company to export, improve exporting capabilities and help enter new export markets.

6 - High Growth Coaching

High growth businesses could get up to 10 days of business coaching over 6-18 months (free, full or part funded).

7 - Improving Your Resource Efficiency

Onsite support provided through local and regional programmes. Loans and grants with advice on environment.

8 Knowledge Transfer Partnerships

Accessing knowledge and skills from Education Institutions and research organisations (part-funded by a grant).

9 Manufacturing Advisory Service

Specialist support with production related issues such as lean processes, supply chain and innovation in manufacturing.

10 Networking for Innovation

Bringing together business, universities, research, finance and technology to stimulate knowledge transfer.

11 Rural Development Programme for England Business Support

Farms and other rural businesses could access funding support to improve competitiveness and environmental sustainability.

12 Understanding Finance for Business

Free advice and support from specialist advisors to ensure small businesses understand the options to grow money.

13 Work Place Training, Including Apprenticeships

Access apprenticeships, work-based training and develop Management and Leadership. Part funded by the Government.

Source: Solutions for Business

Government Funded Business Support: A Guide for Business (published 2011)

The Business Support Simplification Programme had condensed £2.5 billion of tax-funded business support into thirteen boxes, all accessed via Business Link as the first point of contact. A myriad of business support initiatives had been slashed, a process that incurred an estimated £5 million in time / opportunity costs between 2007 and 2009.[76] This action was taken in spite of criticism that a 'one size fits all' offering would be the outcome. Business Link advisers were instructed to send small businesses to these flagship 'products'. PR wise the logo design wasn't a great start and the irony of promoting simplicity on a piece of *red* tape did not go unnoticed.

A credit crunch would test this newfound 'simplicity' to the limit.

CHAPTER TWELVE

RECESS STRESS

2008

"What I want to draw to the House's attention today is the failure of the policies that, in the Government's words, are supposed to be providing 'real help now' to families and businesses struggling with the recession. That slogan is a cruel joke to thousands of people who have lost their jobs, and continue to lose their jobs, while this Government dither and delay."

Mr George Osborne MP, Shadow Chancellor of the Exchequer
House of Commons Debate – 18th March, 2009

On 9th August, 2007, French bank BNP Paribas informed investors they were forbidden to withdraw money from two funds due to difficulties valuing their assets. The bank cited a "complete evaporation of liquidity" in the market as the cause for this crisis. The announcement was the first visible sign that banks had started to refuse to do business with each other. The credit crunch was underway.

The banking crisis created an unprecedented set of trading conditions for businesses. In an effort to save their own organisations the banks rapidly reigned in credit facilities and put pressure on small businesses. For Business Link advisers around the country a significant percentage of their clients now faced financial meltdown. Long held overdraft facilities either evaporated or incurred a new regime of charges. Short-term survival was now the primary objective rather than high growth.

Many businesses had unwisely relied on short term lending to fund long-term commitments, viewing their overdraft as a permanent fixture. This was not necessarily foolish, as no one conceived a banking failure on this scale. Borrowing money for new ventures was virtually impossible, despite banks repeatedly claiming to be "open for business" to anyone who would still listen. Quite suddenly there was simply not as much money about, sales fell, costs went up and access to finance was strangled. This squeeze on credit facilities at such short notice put numerous small and medium sized businesses at risk of failure. The country formally fell into recession during the second half of 2008.

The Government was compelled to intervene. In a fanfare of publicity a series of "Real Help Now" rescue measures were announced to help businesses through the credit crunch. Business Link would be the gateway to this 'new' support. The Real Help Now campaign was greeted with more than a little cynicism from Personal Business Advisers, perplexed that all the support before must have been unreal?

Health Check

In November 2008, the Government announced the launch of a 'new' Business Link product to help businesses "identify and respond positively to the issues faced as a result of the economic downturn." [77]

The free "Health Check" promised a full business review to identify new opportunities and address any challenges brought on by recession. Personal Business Advisers would generate action plans to grow small businesses in difficult times. The more attentive noticed that this 'new' product sounded distinctly like the existing Business Link advisory service. Despite a prominent marketing campaign and promises of additional support, the product was essentially the same.

Each Regional Development Agency was free to interpret the Real Help Now brief as they saw fit and health checks had minor variations from area to area.

In November 2009, the Early Assessment of Business Link Health Checks reported that "in practice, most regions are operating a very similar model for the Health Checks, based on the Intensive Assist model and the terms were seen as interchangeable in some regions. This was mainly due to the similarities of the process." The Health Check product was clearly a tweak and re-brand of the existing service rather than a new government investment to save business. On 12th October, 2009, Ms Rosie Winterton, Minister of State at the Department for Business, Innovation and Skills, confirmed just 894 Business Link employees in the entire country were carrying out health checks. [78]

No additional advisers had been recruited specifically to deliver the scheme. It was business as usual in unusual times.

The Health Check was intensive assistance, delivered turbo. The "Early Assessment" report confirmed that the "face to face meetings with advisers typically last between one and two hours." This shorter intervention didn't mean the Health Check was valueless. Advisers were still using established consultancy tools such as Balanced Scorecard and Forum 21.[79] However, compared to the normal advisory service, the Health Check delivered significantly less time with a business. Small businesses didn't seem to mind. Any help at all is appreciated when knee deep in a financial mire.

On 27th January, 2010, Ms Rosie Winterton announced 79% of businesses accessing the Health Check "were satisfied with the information provided and of those who accessed additional support, 93% were satisfied with this further assistance."[80]

Bail Out

The Business Link advisory support was providing moral support for businesses in a time of need. However, for small businesses the real need was hard currency to get through the hard times intact, not a health check.

The financial rescue stimulus announced by the Government on 14th January, 2009, raised the hopes of many small and medium sized businesses. If you were a high growth potential business, an application for financial assistance would be considered. However, if you were one of the plentiful static state entrepreneurs in the UK, people who run their business to earn a living and not change the world, you weren't on the list and were effectively barred. Business Link advisers, the key referrers to the schemes, judged which businesses constituted high growth. This exclusion clause was attached to all funding within the Real Help for Business package.

Hope 1 – Capital for Enterprise Fund (CfEF)

A new £75 million fund - £25 million from Banks and £50 million from Government funding. Fund makes investments of between £200,000 and £2 million of equity and mezzanine finance. Money can be used to pay off existing debt to free up capital for cash flow and investment.

By September 2009, only five businesses had received investment via the Capital for Enterprise Fund and a total value of £6.15 million had been paid out. Despite the 'Now' promise, and urgency of a credit crisis, the first investment was not actually made until seven months after launch.[81]

"As a commercial fund the investment process for CfEF involves a period of due diligence and negotiation, which involves the fund manager and potential investee company and often existing investors and lenders to the business. The length of time required to complete this can vary significantly in each case and there is no formal target time between an application and investment."

Rosie Winterton MP. Minister of State at the Department for Business, Innovation and Skills. House of Commons Hansard Written Answers 12th October, 2009

Anyone who has experienced Business Angel investment or equity deals knows the truth in this statement. However, it does beg a basic marketing question about managing expectations when talking to your customers. This fund was never going to provide immediate help to the suffering majority, certainly not *"now."*

Hope 2 – Enterprise Finance Guarantee Scheme (EFG)

A Government guarantee of £1 billion to support up to £1.3 billion of bank lending to smaller firms (annual turnover up to £25 million). Businesses struggling to secure the finance they need through normal commercial lending could apply for loans of £1,000 to £1 million with a payback period up to 10 years.

This scheme had already been in existence in the form of Small Firms Loan Guarantee. However, under the Real Help for Businesses Now initiative, the terms and eligibility were relaxed, opening up the scheme to a larger number of small businesses.

Up to 21st August, 2009, loans totalling over £470 million had been offered to over 4,600 businesses.[82]

Hope 3 – <u>Working Capital Scheme (WCS)</u>

Banks provided with up to £10 billion of guarantees covering 50% of risk. This creates a credit line of up to £20 billion of working capital, and frees up finance that banks "must use for new lending" to businesses with a turnover of up to £500 million.

Obviously the most striking observation about the Working Capital Scheme was the barrier to direct applications from small and medium sized businesses. These organisations could not apply for the funding.

Instead, the Government guarantees were offered directly to banks, as an incentive to lend to those most in need. This action was not very reassuring, considering the recent track record of the banking sector.

Hope 4 - <u>Business Payment Support Service</u>

HM Revenue and Customs (HMRC) pledged to work with businesses "facing difficulties in paying taxes" and offered them a chance to "defer 60% of the increase in their 2009-10 business rate bills until 2010-11 and 2011-12."

This element of the Real Help portfolio was widely taken up. It is rare for the immovable HM Revenue and Customs to offer a rate holiday. However, the Government was still in no mood to throw good money after bad. Once again, you had to be a "viable business" to qualify.

"It is important that initiatives designed to provide substantive support to our vital small business sector at a time of global economic challenge work in practice for every small business that needs help. About 66,000 small businesses have had their tax deferred and all will benefit in one way or another from the VAT cut and the extra money that has gone into the economy from tax rebates."

Harriet Harman MP, Leader of the House of Commons

House of Commons Debate Hansard 26th February, 2009

In 2009 alone, the HMRC agreed 240,700 time-to-pay arrangements, putting off payments valued at £4.18 billion.[83]

A number of Regional Development Agencies also contributed to the bail out for small businesses by setting up area specific funds. For example, in the South West a £10 million regional loan fund complemented the national portfolio.[84] This fund was administered much closer to the end customer and the decision making process was six to eight weeks, a positive sprint compared to the national schemes.

Finally, the package included a golden handshake scheme (which offered to pay a company £1,000 to recruit anyone unemployed over six months) and funding to subsidise the take up of apprenticeships.

"The Federation of Small Businesses said Business Link had responded quickly and effectively to the downturn and had put resources into supporting access to finance, helping some of their members through the "finance minefield." The Confederation of British Industry said Business Link had "moved swiftly and decisively" especially with regard to the lack of liquidity available to private sector firms."

House of Commons

North West Regional Committee - First Report 15th July, 2009

Immediate feedback suggested Business Link Operators had reacted in a timely and effective fashion, helping small businesses in their hour of need. This achievement was in spite of an increase in the government contractual targets for Business Links, during the most difficult trading conditions for a generation. The key performance measures rose in both volume and value terms, i.e. the number of businesses expected to grow 15% per annum. Sadly, there weren't so many of those around anymore.

Regardless, the roll out of the "Real Help for Businesses Now" programme was plagued with accusations of delay and duplicity.

Real help for businesses now

Where to find help for your business when you need it.

The Government is taking action to help businesses through the global recession and to ensure they emerge stronger on the other side. This sheet gives you a quick summary of what help is available and where to find it. More details of the full range of support can be found at www.businesslink.gov.uk/realhelp, or call 0845 600 9 006.

Help with business finances

■ Finance from your bank

You may be able to benefit from the Government's *Enterprise Finance Guarantee* if you apply for a loan from your bank. It supports loans of up to £1 million for firms with turnover up to £25 million; you can also convert an existing overdraft into a loan to free up capital.

■ Equity investment

The *Capital for Enterprise Fund* provides equity investment which you can use to pay off existing debt or invest in your business. Call the registration helpline on 0845 459 9780.

To find the right finance for your business, including details of loans available regionally, visit [www.businesslink.gov.uk/realhelp] or speak to an adviser on 0845 600 9 006.

Free guides on managing your cashflow are also available at [www.businesslink.gov.uk/realhelp].

■ More time to pay your tax bill

You may be able to spread tax, National Insurance, VAT, PAYE or other payments over time to help you overcome temporary difficulties. Contact the HMRC Business Payment Support Service on 0845 302 1435.

■ Managing debt

For free, confidential and independent help to deal with business debt problems, call the Business Debtline on 0800 197 6026.

Help with managing your business

■ Business healthcheck

For a free review of your business by a professional adviser who can provide hands-on advice and help you access the full range of government help, call

Business Link on 0845 600 9 006 or visit [www.businesslink.gov.uk/healthcheck].

■ Recruitment and redundancy

From April 2009, you could get an incentive of up to £1000 to recruit a person who has been unemployed for over 6 months, and access to in-work training for them, worth up to £1500. More details will be available soon at [www.businesslink.gov.uk/realhelp].

An interactive guide to help you find alternatives to making redundancies, plus guidance on staff restructuring, is available at [www.businesslink.gov.uk/realhelp].

If you have to make people redundant, Jobcentre Plus helps people at risk of losing their job to start looking for a new one, even before they are made redundant. Visit [www.jobcentreplus.gov.uk/employers].

■ Help with exporting

For help finding the right contacts, navigating local business regulations and raising your company profile in overseas markets, call a UK Trade & Investment adviser on 020 7215 8000 or visit [www.uktradeinvest.gov.uk].

Help with investing for the future

■ Funding and support for training

Train to Gain provides Government funding and free skills advice to businesses, including funding for retraining and access to business-critical training for small and medium-sized firms. Call 0800 01 555 45 or visit [www.traintogain.gov.uk/helping_your_business].

■ Training support for apprentices

You can get full or partial financial support for training apprentices up to the equivalent of A level. Call 0800 015 0600 or visit [www.apprenticeships.org.uk/employers.aspx].

 HM Government

Real Help for Businesses Now (information leaflet)

Published by HM Government February 2009 URN 02/09/Business

A Reality Cheque

The Real Help initiative received national media coverage, championed by Lord Mandelson himself as a significant set of 'new' emergency measures for business. Not surprisingly, the reality was less clear-cut.

Déjà Voodoo

By mid-2009, Business Link advisers had been referring customers to the Solutions for Business products for over 12 months and were more than familiar with that support package. The news of "new" help was greeted with a degree of cynicism from those who saw this rescue package as fundamentally a re-marketing exercise.

"Much of what is offered under the Real Help Now banner is a simple re-branding of pre-existing products; to that end the Real Help Now documentation is a useful tool for bringing information about sources of support into one place, but offers few new solutions for business."

Memorandum from the Confederation of British Industry - House of Commons North West Regional Committee Written Evidence, 31st July, 2009

The Government faced accusations of re-branding previously announced funding. For example, the Enterprise Finance Guarantee had been available for a number of years prior to the credit crunch (in the original Small Firms Loan Guarantee guise). The decision to relax the qualifying criteria undoubtedly opened up this scheme to a wider market, but it was hardly novel.

In many ways, government spin was irrelevant to entrepreneurs, who just wanted some help and responded immediately to a call to action. By February 2010, over 110,000 businesses had completed the 'Health Check' process.[85] The added publicity created a spike in new customers coming to Business Link, when small and medium sized businesses were most in need.

Advisers and businesses were thankful for that alone. Opposition politicians would be less forgiving.

Jam tomorrow, possibly the day after?

The most serious criticism of the Real Help Now campaign was directed at the financial schemes. It was not the structure of the funding that caused disquiet, rather the time taken to release the cash to small businesses.

The 'new' funding was designed to bail out viable organisations facing a working capital and cash crisis. As most businesses will know at one time or another, this situation is precarious at best and immediate. Weeks rather than months are critical to continue trading.

"There is a bit of frustration. Business Link and the RDA have their hands tied behind their back because they can only operate at the same speed that central government operate. A classic example is the Venture Capital Loan Fund. I know Business Link has been geared up since January to deliver that and the latest estimate is that it will be launched in June. It is almost fighting with one arm tied behind its back. It was an issue over the Treasury signing off that delayed that."

Damien Waters, Regional Director of the CBI North West

House of Commons North West Regional Committee Evidence 15th June, 2009

Even though the business support solutions had been through a "vigorous" simplification process, the wheels of central government and workings of the banking sector looked somewhat less fluid.

In fairness, securing business finance is not a 'computer says yes or no' decision. The timescales were always going to be months rather than weeks. Lenders must ensure due diligence is completed on applicants and that the approval process is strictly followed. After all this was credit crunch, not Christmas lunch.

The real issue was a failure to manage expectations effectively when the big announcements were made in the media. So much so that the Confederation of British Industry even went so far as to express their "sympathy" for Business Link and the RDA who were dealing with the fall out from a "whole wave of announcements and policies that take a long time to filter down."[86]

Dealing with dissatisfied customers is inconsequential compared to the plight of small businesses, who slowly realised the knight in shining armour was tied up in red tape and would not be riding to the rescue. On 10th March, 2009, Conservative Member of Parliament David Jones spoke for many when he asked whether "this a case *not* of real help now, but of jam tomorrow, or possibly the day after?"[87]

Three Monkeys

During 2009, the banks were under a sustained attack from both the Government and media whilst trying to secure their own financial stability and long-term future. The baying masses contended that lenders had taken unnecessary risks and gambled wildly, rather than invested prudently. Ironically, in this already vitriolic atmosphere, the Government started to lambaste the same institutions for being too cautious and miserly with their money. Banks are independent businesses (at least they were!) whose Directors are accountable in law to act in the best interests of their Company and shareholders. It is hardly surprising that some of the commands coming down from government appeared to fall upon deaf ears.

"The 'Real help now' package that the Government have put in place shows their determination to help small businesses, but the banks remain stubbornly resistant to co-operating with what has been put in place. Businesses in my area describe interest rates being held stubbornly high or increased, bank charges being imposed without warning and a requirement for 100 per cent security despite the fact that loans are covered by the guarantee scheme."

Clive Efford MP – Labour Party
House of Commons Debate 19th March, 2009

In this same House of Commons debate, Ian Pearson, Economic Secretary to the Treasury, acknowledged the Government "cannot stand in the shoes of the banks that have to make commercial lending decisions on the basis of their assessment and pricing of risk. That is what would be expected of any functioning economy." However, he then assured his Honourable Friends that the Government would "rigorously monitor the situation." A case of damned if you do, damned if you don't for the banking sector?

In February 2009, Lord Mandelson confirmed "400 businesses had received loans under the new Enterprise Finance Guarantee, with more than £40 million lent by 23 high street lenders in the UK."[88] Barclays had lent £12 million and Lloyds £4.5 million, not huge sums in banking terms but enough to evidence at least that the banks were taking tentative steps to engage with the Real Help Now initiative.

In reality, the banks were still lending significant sums of money to small and medium sized businesses, but *only* if the applicants satisfied revised, and much more stringent, approval criteria.

Speaking Up

On 14th January, 2009, Lord Mandelson, Secretary of State for Business, Innovation and Skills (BIS), made a series of pledges to businesses in the UK.

"We know that some companies are struggling to secure the finance they need, not because of any failure in their business but due to the tougher credit conditions. That is why we have designed a package of measures addressing different forms of credit and providing real help for businesses."

"I want to make sure that when we intervene, we intervene in a way that is really effective, really targets genuine business needs in a way that gives value for money from the Government and the taxpayers' point of view, and is genuinely going to help businesses in what is a very difficult credit situation."

"The support package we are launching today builds on the commitments we made in November's Pre-Budget report. It addresses the cash flow, credit and capital needs of businesses. We are offering specific solutions - not a blanket subsidy."

"Our scheme will be targeted, it will be thought through, it will be funded and it will be focused on those businesses that we want to *support most of all.*"

Lord Mandelson, Secretary of State for Business, Innovation and Skills
Real Help Now Press Conference, London 14th January, 2009.

Behind the rhetoric of this battling rescue speech was definitely help for businesses. Yes, a good proportion of the support already existed in one form or another. And yes, the new financial initiatives were relatively complex and time intensive to travel for any small business. However, as Lord Mandelson added, we were "in unique times and uncharted territory."

Business confidence was in need of an urgent boost, be it real or smoke and mirrors. At least someone in the country was talking up the chances of recovery and sending out a message to a fairly shell shocked small business population that they were not alone. Lord Mandelson would be just about the last politician to do so with any conviction.

The Real Help Now campaign cost £1.4 million, spending incurred from existing government budgets. As the Labour Party's Liam Byrne MP (the former Treasury Chief Secretary) said in his infamous leaving note, "I'm afraid to tell you there's no money left." What choices did the Labour Government have but to rebrand existing assets, make future guarantees and try to increase market awareness?

Despite best efforts, the subsequent failure to stimulate a business recovery delivered anti-interventionists all the ammunition needed to blast the Business Link advisory service into oblivion.

CHAPTER THIRTEEN

DRAGONS' BREATH

2008

"The existing variety of approaches, policies, systems and business models across and within the nine regions, when the issues facing small business and the questions that need to be answered are virtually identical, is absurd."

"As a general rule Government should not provide business advice."

Small Business and Government: The Richard Report
Submission to Shadow Cabinet (Conservative) by Doug Richard
8th May, 2008

On 8th May, 2008, the Conservative Party published the Richard Report, their Small Business Task Force review of business support in England. The Task Force was led by none other than Doug Richard, the successful technology entrepreneur from America, notorious for his time on the television show Dragon's Den.

The release of the Richard Report was greeted with a short burst of media attention, but soon fell off the radar of small businesses. Not so the Conservative Party, who three years on would use this template as the foundation of Prime Minister David Cameron's business support policy.

Task Mask

The opening proclamation in the Richard Report is an unambiguous claim of complete political neutrality. The report had been "written by independent business people of all political persuasions and none." The recommendations were "equally applicable whoever is in government. This is not an ideological report rooted in any political philosophic tradition."[89]

This opening gambit clearly pitched the report as a manifesto for small business by small business. Yet it is evidently impossible to discuss issues on government provision of business support without being ideological. Intervention is by nature a political, divisive topic.

The Task Force attacked the Labour led Government for not knowing "its own limits", stating categorically that government should "not seek to intervene itself" to help small businesses. The Labour Party's policies and spending on business support were accused of being "motivated primarily by social and political policies and not based on the needs of business." The authors then took a quantum leap off the political fence by claiming the Labour Government was "operating a socially re-distributive policy in the guise of small business assistance." These claims may or may not be true, but they certainly aren't apolitical. Despite the paper claim of independence, the Conservative funded review still raised dramatic and thought provoking ideas on improving small business.

204

The release of the Richard Report went largely unnoticed by the majority of small businesses, if only because the Conservatives were in Opposition and their policies were not yet a clear and present alternative. However, the Richard Report would ultimately impact on all small and medium sized businesses.

Doug's Dossier

The Richard Report was rich with evidence (statistics) to justify an all out assault on public funded business support in 2008.

"The current Government is presiding over a system, which is overly complex, ineffective and undirected. Some three thousand business support schemes are being run by over two thousand public bodies and their contractors at a direct cost of at least £2.5 billion. Total public expenditure spent on supporting small business is now more correctly estimated to be £10- £12 billion, and much is wasted."

Small Business and Government: The Richard Report

Submission to Shadow Cabinet (Conservative) by Doug Richard 8th May, 2008

The Task Force commissioned Boys Smith Consulting Ltd to examine the effect, if any, publicly funded regional support was having on businesses. Their investigation was targeted squarely at the main players, Regional Development Agencies, Business Links and Learning and Skills Councils. Rather unsurprisingly, their findings reported regional variations in spending on small businesses, which wasn't exactly a revelation. The creation of Regional Development Agencies in the first place had been to permit autonomous deployment of resources for differing local needs.

The claims of unfair distribution of funds continued. For each small business in the North East, public funding of £1,068 per annum was invested on direct support. Contrast this figure with the East of England, where each business had to make do with the miserly sum of £109. Apolitically, of course, the Task Force was implying the Government of the day had created a North / South business-divide. The spotlight then fell darkly over the Business Links.

"A DTI-backed case study of three English regions found that 66 per cent of Business Link services were 'signposting' (to other support) and that 60 per cent of spending on SMEs in the regions was under the control of Business Link Providers. It is difficult to understand how so much funding can be spent on signposting. It is as though we have created a labyrinth of services that are so complex that we have had to create a further service whose primary unintentional remit is to decipher them."

Small Business and Government: The Richard Report

Submission to Shadow Cabinet (Conservative) by Doug Richard 8th May, 2008

The authors once again credited this confusion to the Regional Development Agencies who had designed "individual responses to their common purpose." The Richard Report accused the Government of putting "business support firmly in the policy context and political control of RDAs", who created "distinctive flavours" rather than a "pure" form of business support.

The Task Force evidence for change kept on coming. 33.5 percent of every pound spent on SME business support from central government was "lost to administration." Only 34 percent of local business support schemes were evaluated in any way, the remainder being unaccountable.

Many of the Richard Report figures were at odds with recent surveys and audited performance data about Business Link. The Regional Development Agencies reported over 590,000 businesses received Business Link assistance during 2007 to 2008.[90] Over the same period, Business Link services achieved a customer satisfaction rating of 89.7 percent. This figure was 92 percent for website users.[91]

Omission of this data in the Richard Report is noteworthy in itself.

Back to the Future

"We feel that the best mechanism to determine who provides the advice that the small business owners desire is the customers themselves. Placing these providers in competition with all other advisors and making the small business owner pay for the advice will immediately create a marketplace that will survive or fail based solely on its value."

Small Business and Government: The Richard Report
Submission to Shadow Cabinet (Conservative) by Doug Richard 8th May, 2008

This simple paragraph would sweep away 20 years of business support policy. If you were a small business that was not prepared to put your hand in your pocket to pay for support, you would by default be deemed unenterprising and expected to survive or thrive on your own. Those with guts to invest would be deserving of any government support in the future vision.

This philosophy overlooked the possibility that many small businesses do not relish the appointment of consultants and remain suspicious of promised returns. Was this a failure of the Business Link mission to promote consultancy or an inconvenient constant in the mindset of small business? After all, the vast majority of entrepreneurs remain cash strapped and consequently risk-sensitive during their early years of trading. The Task Force had no such reservations.

"We believe that the Conservative Government should focus its efforts on enabling the provision of information, not advice. There is no need for Government advisors to try and compete with private and third sector agencies. Government should instead work through business experts, existing institutions and current programmes that could be reinforced rather than being reinvented."

Small Business and Government: The Richard Report
Submission to Shadow Cabinet (Conservative) by Doug Richard 8th May, 2008

**Small Business
and Government:**

The Richard Report

Submission to Shadow Cabinet
Doug Richard

Foreword

As an entrepreneur, I believe strongly in the value of entrepreneurialism and innovation and the role they can play in improving the quality of all our lives.

As an American living and working in Britain, I believe this country has a significant role to play in the rapid globalisation of enterprise we are living through.

That is why I was delighted to be invited by David Cameron to Chair this Task Force to look at the way in which business support is delivered in the UK, and to suggest improvements.

This is a report commissioned by and written for the Conservatives, but written by independent business people of all political persuasions and none. Personally, I have no Party affiliation. For that matter I am not even entitled to vote in the UK. This is important because the members of this Task Force unanimously agree that our critique and recommendations are based on a combination of factual evidence, personal experience and advice from the business community, and are equally applicable whoever is in Government. This is not an ideological report rooted in any political philosophic tradition.

We hope it is read and - more importantly - acted upon in that spirit.

Douglas Richard
Chairman

Foreword taken from Small Business and Government: The Richard Report

Submission to Shadow Cabinet (Conservative) by Doug Richard 8th May, 2008

The Richard Report was adamant that Business Link was an expensive duplication of existing provision and an unnecessary interference in the affairs of small business.

A Very Free Market

The Richard Report suggested serious deficiencies in the existing provision of business support. Government business support schemes had led to something of a "feeding frenzy" amongst the big public sector consultancies, and an explosion in new "providers of business support." The Task Force voiced a widespread concern amongst consultants that the Government of the day was surreptitiously "sponsoring" a tax-funded "parallel market."

The authors went further and questioned the integrity (even legality) of the Government bidding process to be part of this subsidised market, stating categorically that tendering for contracts had been "far from transparent."

"Companies who have been awarded work on one project, which is then renewed, describe being told that the job will have to be tendered 'but you will win it', which can only mean hundreds of hours of time wasted by other bidders in a sham bid designed only to comply with tender regulations."

Small Business and Government: The Richard Report

Submission to Shadow Cabinet (Conservative) by Doug Richard 8th May, 2008

The Richard Report stated that, "providers of support services" that were good enough to sell their services direct, avoided the hassle of working within government schemes. The implication being that those already working on these contracts were deficient in some way.

Consultancies can typically charge anything between £100 and £5,000 a day, depending on their capability and experience. If you are a small business you may well enter at the bottom of the market, where the value is theoretically lower. As a business grows so does propensity to engage more knowledgeable consultancies and ability to afford fees. Return on investment (hopefully!) rises in line with ability to pay higher day rates. In reality, the impact consultants make to a business does not always rise in line with the day rate.

The Business Link mission was to get reticent entrepreneurs on the first step of the knowledge ladder, to remove barriers to consultancy and stimulate the transfer of knowledge within the private sector. The Richard Report was resolute that the private sector needed no such stimulus, as quality checks and service were already fit for purpose.

"The approach we are advocating would increase the choice, competitiveness and accountability of business support providers, to the benefit of all."

"In a free market, a business advisor will look very hard at a company's prospects before even taking on basic fee-paid work, because for any real business the investment of time in a client, even paid time, represents a significant investment of itself."

Small Business and Government: The Richard Report

Submission to Shadow Cabinet (Conservative) by Doug Richard 8th May, 2008

Private sector consultants are not charities. Consultancy had always been a two-tier market, divided on propensity to pay. Removing subsidised advisory services would not impact upon entrepreneurs willing and able to invest £1,000 plus a day in consultancy. It would hurt the majority of small businesses that want to do better but do not yet feel ready to embrace consultancy.

The Richard Report promised "huge cost savings" as one of the main benefits of their new approach, presumably for the Government and not small business.

Reinventing the Wheel

"There are already a variety of well-established support services run by organisations such as Local Enterprise Agencies and Chambers of Commerce, which bring together qualified advisers with a business background, an established local reputation, and support from the local business community and local authorities."

Small Business and Government: The Richard Report

Submission to Shadow Cabinet (Conservative) by Doug Richard 8th May, 2008

For over 15 years, I have worked in and around both Enterprise Agencies and Chambers of Commerce. The common challenge in the majority of these businesses is access to resources. Typically, these organisations generated revenue from membership subscriptions, training, events and consultancy. However, the main income for many of these organisations came from support contracts, won in the public sector. Enterprise Agencies, for many years, held a virtual monopoly on Business Link start up support contracts. They were successful bidders in the same "parallel market" that the Richard Report described as won by providers whose "credentials in the free market are questionable at best and sometimes non-existent."

The ability of Enterprise Agencies and Chambers of Commerce to be enterprising is not in doubt. Nor is the respect they rightly warrant. But the one thing these organisations never were is adviser heavy, a fact plain to see for anyone who has walked into a local branch outside London, Manchester or Birmingham.

In 2011, Lord Heseltine highlighted this lack of resource within Chambers, by citing public law status as the one thing he would go back and change, in any other name the introduction of a Chamber tax on business.[92] This legal obligation would inflate the wealth of this historic organisation, financing a powerful business support body for small business from within their ranks. In this scenario government would have no cause to intervene.

211

"It means that businesses (must) register with their Chamber, and the Chambers therefore much richer, and can give far more impressive support, which they do on the continent. If you travel overseas you see the support the Chambers give to German or French industry, it's amazing."

The Rt Hon the Lord Heseltine CH

Interview with author at Haymarket Media Group Head Office, Hammersmith, London

8th June, 2011

According to Lord Heseltine, public law status is a sensitive issue that remains unpalatable to those steadfast against intervention. "The climate here would be very hostile to it, including the climate of organisations that claim to represent small businesses."

I have the highest respect for both Enterprise Agencies and Chambers of Commerce. I have been part of the help they deliver to small businesses and have seen first hand the quality of their people. However, the suggestion their existence makes Business Links superfluous is difficult to accept when you consider the scale of demand. In excess of 750,000 organisations asked for assistance from Business Links during 2009 / 2010.[93]

You've Been Framed

"The Conservative Party's Head of Policy, Oliver Letwin MP, recently spoke about the need for a shift from a 'provision-based paradigm' to a 'framework-based paradigm'. We believe that this is a model which well describes the way in which government should interact with small businesses: to enable a framework for support, but not to seek to intervene itself, unless reasonable access to advice and support is not practically possible."

Small Business and Government: The Richard Report

Submission to Shadow Cabinet (Conservative) by Doug Richard 8th May, 2008

The Task Force threw their full support behind this new framework, founded on light touch facilitation rather than heavy-handed intervention.

Dot Gov Love

"Initial business information should be separated from advice, with the former provided as a single, web-based exchange replacing the existing regional information and advice services. This portal should be funded by Government and it should operate as an open exchange able to signpost enquirers to the advice and support they need."

Small Business and Government: The Richard Report
Submission to Shadow Cabinet (Conservative) by Doug Richard 8th May, 2008

The Task Force, led by a technological entrepreneur, had proposed a website to fill any void left by the closure of a national advisory service. If you were a small business, the Task Force had decided you posed "pedestrian challenges and questions" and that it was "absurd" that nine regions were dealing with these "virtually identical" questions in different ways.

"The issues on which small business owners regularly seek advice are generally similar, regardless of geographical location. We believe that this points towards a single system of information... via the shortest route possible."

Small Business and Government: The Richard Report
Submission to Shadow Cabinet (Conservative) by Doug Richard 8th May, 2008

A large percentage of questions asked by small businesses are, indeed, common to all organisations. However, an online vision omits the key advantage of personal business, the opportunity to be asked a question back. The question is often just a symptom of a far greater problem or opportunity, one that has not yet presented itself to the business concerned, and may never do so. The Task Force would have us believe online communities and email can challenge a small business WHY they are looking for information in the first place and ensure any answers are fit for purpose and best value, not just part of a one way conveyor belt of data.

It is not disrespectful to anyone to raise unconsciousness incompetence, a universal issue affecting us all. This is when an entrepreneur does not understand, or know how to do something, and more critically does not recognise this deficit. This is common to all people, not just entrepreneurs, but is a significant barrier to small businesses reaching their full potential. If you do not know you have a problem, how can you address it until it is too late? Without knowing the right question to ask, how can you get the right answer? You will get *an* answer, but at what cost.

In today's cash poor economy, many are quick to assume people are a disposable commodity. Push button downloading of information is well suited to the Web and offers cost / speed savings. However, one-way communication is contrary to the principles of knowledge transfer, understanding and converting information into sustained learning and improvement. This issue is unintentionally highlighted further by the Richard Report itself, which holds up the British Library Business and IP Centre as a benchmark solution to this challenge.

The Task Force recommended similar centres should be opened around the UK. The British Library model was "offering free access to business and intellectual property in one place in London with impartial experts to guide people to the information that they need." The British Library was rightly credited for helping over 30,000 small businesses over a 2 year period, running 250 workshops and providing one to one mentoring and coaching sessions ("free or highly subsidised"). The Richard Report believed "the strength of the British Library's approach is that it has focused on providing access to key information supported by *expertise*." The key element to success was "impartial experts to guide people to the information that they need" – not that they want. The British Library model was *not* a self-serving online solution with only administrators to guide you.

Three years later the single business information service implemented by the coalition Government would have no army of experts to challenge small businesses. Instead, a garrison of guides would be employed in a national Call Centre, remote helpers with the express directive to help users find the right information on the website and not to intervene.

Key information supported by navigation, *not* expertise.

Pure unambiguous self-interest

"Creating an information exchange that lets experts from the private sector provide support either commercially or in return for exposure to their expertise, would have the dual effect of having the experts that entrepreneurs already trust provide the material, and reducing burden on Government to support small business in an area where it is neither trusted nor expert."

Small Business and Government: The Richard Report
Submission to Shadow Cabinet (Conservative) by Doug Richard 8th May, 2008

In the Richard Report vision, the source to replace government funded advice would flow freely from small businesses themselves.

"It is possible that the most valuable advice may actually be provided without recourse to any professional advisor at all. Simply by harnessing the power of really well managed networking technology such as that behind Facebook, You tube and other online communities, first class business advice can be made available to people who wouldn't otherwise know how to access it. What would be the incentive for people to be part of this network? Pure, unambiguous self-interest."

Small Business and Government: The Richard Report
Submission to Shadow Cabinet (Conservative) by Doug Richard 8th May, 2008

The Task Force rightly pointed out that "running a small business is often a lonely pastime" and cited the importance of networks as a key way to overcome this isolation. The Richard Report concluded "most small business people would be only too glad to provide advice on issues they have dealt with in the past to fellow entrepreneurs." According to the Richard Report, it is this faith in the self-interest and eternal goodwill of small businesses that would fill any void left by dismantling the Business Link advisory service. A nation of knowledge philanthropists, willing to freely donate hard earned lessons (often costly) to help another.

The Task Force was proposing a Utopian vision for better business. If you will, a call to working businessmen of all Counties, UNITE!

The same businessmen widely acknowledged as being time poor, pressurised, stressed and constantly fighting for competitive advantage against their peers.

The Ebay Way

"As for ensuring quality advice and service, we believe this will best be achieved by enabling small businesses to rank the service they received using the web-based exchange, rather than Government trying to establish new quality standards. The best example of a web ranking system is the vendor ranking system on e-bay, which permits buyers and sellers both to rank each other and to provide commentary in their own defence."

Small Business and Government: The Richard Report

Submission to Shadow Cabinet (Conservative) by Doug Richard 8th May, 2008

The Richard Report proposed a "system of online customer feedback and buyer and seller grading" to manage any consultancy register. Self-regulation would enable businesses to select from a larger pool of providers and access a "higher calibre" of advice. The new system would be more transparent, more accountable, ensuring the consultants themselves were "exposed to the same rigour of the market", driving up standards.

"Business support providers would be able to offer their services and stake their claims, active buyer and seller feedback would be a condition of use, replacing unaccountable and intermittent accreditation by Government. This would directly empower small businesses."

Small Business and Government: The Richard Report

Submission to Shadow Cabinet (Conservative) by Doug Richard 8th May, 2008

The concept of customer feedback is not a new idea and has been considered in the previous incarnations of consultancy registers. However, past attempts floundered as it was felt consultants would be reluctant to expose their brands to very public comment by very unpredictable customers. As a predominantly intangible product, the value of consultancy is extremely subjective. This issue is compounded further as any return on investment can take years to present itself.

In addition, there is the Mexican stand off effect found in Ebay, where buyer and seller value their online rating as an asset, so much so that they agree not to disagree, an effect which can inadvertently mask negative feedback.

Whatever the reservations about public ratings, previous government attempts have failed to create a comprehensively populated Consultancy register with a high attrition rate.

The Richard Report was adamant that the removal of Business Link would promote less "transactional distortion" when a small business selects a supplier. Based on these assumptions alone, the new Ebay way must be worth a try.

Schools Doubt

"Creating a more entrepreneurial culture in the UK is vital, both to our economy and to enabling millions of people to fulfil their personal potential. We propose a number of reforms, which emphasise the primacy of hands-on experience. Enterprise and entrepreneurship are best understood when practiced, not taught. In Norway, this approach has proven highly successful, where the proportion of school students setting up in business is double that of the general population. We believe the UK can learn from the key elements of this programme, not least enabling there to be a business in every school."

Small Business and Government: The Richard Report

Submission to Shadow Cabinet (Conservative) by Doug Richard 8th May, 2008

The most radical element of the Richard Report had nothing to do with business support. The Small Business Task Force set their sights on deficiencies in the education system, pointing to Norway as the way forward. The Task Force proposed a number of key changes to business studies in schools and colleges.

- Stop treating enterprise as a separate subject and spread this learning across the entire curriculum.

- Encourage the creation of school-based businesses run by students and teachers.

- Help schools partner with local businesses to bring in "outside know-how" and show students what enterprise looks and feels like.

- Each school should be given autonomy on how they integrate enterprise into their own teaching.

If being entrepreneurial is a state of mind, exposing young people to this way of thinking at the earliest age possible must be an advantage. The report lauded the Norway approach, where it was policy that "local and regional state agencies spend ten percent of their economic development budgets on the training and support of enterprise education."

The Richard Report acknowledged the need to nurture enterprise amongst the 4.4 million existing small businesses. However, with the business in every school goal they aimed directly at the source of the sickness, prevention not cure for a next generation of entrepreneurs.

Broken Link

"Government Business Links (BL) have sought to provide competing services and the regionalisation of BL has also fostered a subsidiary system of Government-awarded local monopolies on business advice.

Small Business and Government: The Richard Report
Submission to Shadow Cabinet (Conservative) by Doug Richard 8th May, 2008

Peppered throughout the Richard Report is an exhaustive list of statistics and sound bites designed to condemn the Government of the day's business support policy. The content of the Richard Report is valuable and relevant to all small businesses. However, it is a folly to claim the document does not sit on the right or left of political opinion. A century old debate on whether government has the right to stick their nose in the affairs of a free market capitalist economy is testament to this fact. Whilst the use of statistics could be accused of being selective and excluding data that might counter a case against intervention, there is no doubt that the demand for change in Business Links was valid. The seismic change advocated by Doug Richard and the other members of the Task Force was unambiguous. Withdraw the hand of intervention, dismantle existing infrastructure, and shunt government policy back to a laissez-faire paradigm.

The Dragon's teeth had been planted. The subsequent credit crunch on public finances just accelerated the process of change.

CHAPTER FOURTEEN

PRISK END

2010 to 2011

"Obviously I regret any redundancies that result from either that decision or others. Clearly, none of us relishes that prospect, but Business Link was widely criticised by the businesses for which it was designed. It was not an effective system, nor was it cost-effective for the taxpayer, so the Minister of State, Department for Business, Innovation and Skills, my Hon. Friend the Member for Hertford and Stortford (Mr Mark Prisk MP), is developing a new model, based essentially on website advice."

Dr. Vince Cable MP, Secretary of State for Business, Innovation and Skills
House of Commons Hansard Debates 28th October, 2010

In May 2010, the Conservative / Liberal Democrat coalition was formed and took power of the country. The new Administration immediately declared their intent to reduce the threat of budget deficit by putting responsibility for business growth firmly back at the door of private enterprise. The state of public finances meant the Government was incapable of buying their way out of trouble. As a result, the coalition Government had little choice but to plead with businesses to save the day - small, medium and large.

The intervention debate intensified as the Global economy continued to flounder. In the face of unprecedented trading conditions, a £150 million budget for Business Links seemed inadequate and unlikely to tackle nationwide issues, a force of two thousand advisers trying to stimulate a business population of almost five million. Add in an ideological influx from the incumbent coalition Government and Business Link's time was up.

Wrecked Reputation

"As many people on this side of the House who have run small businesses will know, the problem with Business Link was that it was a very ineffective system of business support. It has now been replaced, and in future small businesses will have access, through mentoring, to other business people, rather than to those who serviced Business Link, which was not a successful scheme."

Dr. Vince Cable MP, Secretary of State for Business, Innovation and Skills
House of Commons Hansard Debate – 9th February, 2011

During 2010 and 2011, a series of announcements were made by Dr. Vince Cable MP (Secretary of State for Business, Innovation and Skills) and Mark Prisk MP (Minister for Small Business), criticising Business Link performance and proclaiming the network to be an expensive failure.

On 17th June, 2010, Lord Sugar himself offered his services as a Government adviser on the issue. Nine months later, after "reviewing the future of the Business Link Centres", Lord Sugar's own conclusions were damning. "To be perfectly frank, apart from meeting a nice bunch of people, there was no real business advice dished out other than simple stuff you could pick up and learn for yourself by going on the Internet."[94]

Shortly afterward, on 6th July, 2010, Mark Prisk MP announced that £2.26 of additional growth was generated by every tax pound spent on Business Link, albeit he then conceded in the same speech that the web and advisor service were "creating significant benefits to businesses through hours saved and reduced cost of regulation compliance."[95]

Again, no one attempted to explain why a failed Business Link was still engaging in excess of 750,000 businesses year on year.[96]

These announcements not only created reaction in the media and business forums, but also caused significant reverberations within Business Links themselves. The Government hailed the demise of Business Link long before details were formally communicated to staff or management.

In the face of persistent criticism, the silence from Business Link Operators was deafening, as these private contractors sought to secure their place on the future map of business support. With the prospect of new contracts to bid for, it would have been commercial suicide for Business Link Operators to challenge any new hand that might feed them. The result was a one-way media mauling for the Business Link brand and it's people.

The closure of the Business Link advisory service took 18 months in the end. During this period a swathe of advisory staff were made redundant. A number of settlements were paid from the closing Government contracts (a phenomenon not unique to Business Link). On November 25th, 2011, after 17 years in the field, the Personal Business Adviser ceased to exist as a service. If you were a small business, Business Link advisers were past. Only the future of business support mattered now.

Forces of Stagnation

"If we do not act now, jobs will be lost, our country will become poorer and we will find it difficult to afford the public services we all want. If we do not wake up to the world around us, our standard of living will fall, not rise. We literally cannot afford to go on like this. The Government has wasted little time in starting what needs to be done."

Dr. Vince Cable, Secretary of State for Business, Innovation and Skills

George Osborne MP, Chancellor of the Exchequer

Foreword from The Plan for Growth, HM Treasury and BIS - March 2011

The coalition Government declared four main goals for business post-New Labour; create the most competitive tax regime in the G20, make the UK one of the best places in Europe to be in business, encourage investment and exports for a "more balanced economy" and create a flexible and better educated workforce.[97]

This desire for balance would have a direct impact on all small businesses. The Government believed business support in the past had been centred on just a handful of sectors and regions. The results were pockets of under achievement where entire regions were "increasingly reliant on the public sector."[98] A few lucky sectors for growth would continue to receive tailored support from the Government. Healthcare and life sciences, advanced engineering, construction, creative industries, retail, business services, space industry and tourism would all benefit from additional measures.

The new "Plan for Growth" recognised the importance of different sectors, but sought to eliminate expensive public sector dependency. The removal of "barriers that get in the way of sustainable private-sector led growth" would be more controversial. However, the issue was not for debate.

"Those who oppose these reforms are the forces of stagnation, who would commit our country to decline."

Dr. Vince Cable, Secretary of State for Business, Innovation and Skills
George Osborne MP, Chancellor of the Exchequer
Foreword from The Plan for Growth, HM Treasury and BIS - March 2011

A state of urgency had been declared. Anyone who had a counter view was effectively branded an enemy of the business state.

Enter Prize

In the 2011 budget, Chancellor of the Exchequer George Osborne MP announced the formation of 21 new Enterprise Zones to tackle the issue of public sector dependency.

The strategy was not a new one. In 1980, Chancellor of the day Geoffrey Howe had first introduced Enterprise Zones under the Thatcher Government to tackle acute unemployment and areas of economic weakness. Back then the London Docklands was selected as one of less than 30 areas to receive rate relief and a relaxed planning process (an area transformed within a generation).

The Coalition tabled similar incentives for businesses to relocate to the new needy regions, agreeing to rubber stamp 21 areas that had "missed out in the last 10 years."[99] Each location would range between 50 and 150 hectares (approximately the size of Hyde Park).

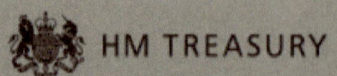

HM TREASURY

BIS
Department for Business
Innovation & Skills

The Plan for Growth

Foreword

This Plan for Growth is an urgent call for action.

Britain has lost ground in the world's economy, and needs to catch up.

If we do not act now, jobs will be lost, our country will become poorer and we will find it difficult to afford the public services we all want. If we do not wake up to the world around us, our standard of living will fall, not rise.

In the last decade other nations have worked hard to make their economies more competitive. They have reduced their business tax rates, removed barriers to enterprise, invested in their infrastructure, improved their education systems, reformed welfare and increased their exports.

Sadly the reverse has happened in Britain over the last ten years. The UK economy stopped saving, investing and exporting and instead turned to a model of growth that failed. It resulted in rising levels of debt, over-leveraged banks, an unsustainable property boom, and a budget deficit that was forecast to be the largest of any of the world's twenty leading economies. Continuously rising but unaffordable government spending disguised the fact that it was an unsustainable economic boom, with the economy becoming steadily more unbalanced, less competitive and less prepared to meet the challenges of the future.

The facts today are staring Britain in the face. We've gone from having the 3rd lowest corporate tax in the EU-15 to having the 7th highest. In the World Economic Forum's Global Competitiveness Index, we've fallen from 4th to 12th. In education, the foundation of economic success, we have slipped back. In international rankings of excellence in maths, we've fallen from 8th to 28th, in science from 4th to 16th. Manufacturing has halved as a share of our economy, and 50 per cent of all manufacturing jobs have been lost. Our share of world exports has fallen from 4.4 per cent in 2000 to 2.8 per cent in 2009. These trends are not inevitable for an advanced economy: look at Germany whose share of world exports was 9.0 per cent in 2009 compared with 8.5 per cent in 2000. Not only do we export just a third as much as Germany, we even lie behind the Netherlands, a country a third our size.

The consequence of this failure over the last decade to confront the causes of our relative economic decline is clear. Our economy has become more and more unbalanced. The gap between the prosperity of the South East and the rest of the UK has grown, as has the gap between the richest in our society and the poorest. This is the case even as government spending has grown to equal about half of the entire national economic output, paid for by our highest peacetime budget deficit.

We literally cannot afford to go on like this.

Britain has to earn its way in the modern world. We have to become much more productive so we can be a leading high tech, highly skilled economy. We must build a new model of economic growth – where instead of borrowing from the rest of the world, we invest and we save and we export. Our economy must become more balanced.

Foreword from The Plan for Growth. Published by HM Treasury and Department for Business, Innovation and Skills in March 2011 (P1)

Private sector growth must take the place of government deficits, and prosperity must be shared across all parts of the UK. We want to remain the world's leading centre for financial services, yes; but we should determine to become a world-leader in, for example, advanced manufacturing, life sciences, creative industries, green energy and non-financial business services.

None of this will be easy to achieve. Difficult, far-reaching changes are needed to make our economy more competitive, the education of our children more effective, and government spending more productive.

The Government has wasted little time in starting what needs to be done. We have set out a credible plan to tackle the budget deficit and bring economic stability. We have set in place annual reductions that will give us the lowest business tax rate in the G7, and reduced taxes on jobs for low and middle earners. We have protected the science budget so we can remain a magnet for technological leadership. We have found funding for a Green Investment Bank so we can get on with building a low carbon future. We are investing in the apprenticeships and innovation centres that industry needs. We have embarked on major reforms of our school, university, welfare, pension and health systems, to make them fit for the demands of the future. Those who oppose these reforms are the forces of stagnation who would commit our country to decline.

But even all this is not enough. We now have to step up a gear. Our economy needs to become much more dynamic, less burdened by pointless barriers, and retooled for a high tech future, if we are going to create the jobs and prosperity we need for the next generation.

We should never again allow our taxes to become uncompetitive, or drive valued entrepreneurs from our shores. If other nations are turning out smarter school and university students, we have to make sure ours are smarter still. We have to tear down the barriers to enterprise and economic development. Britain should be producing businesses that out-compete, out-smart and out-pace the rest of the world.

That is what this Plan for Growth is all about.

None of it is without controversy – all of it involves choices about our priorities.

But the alternative is to accept Britain's economic decline and falling standards of living for our population.

That is not a future we have to settle for.

In the world's race to the top, Britain can come out first.

Vince Cable
Secretary of State for Business,
Innovation and Skills

George Osborne
Chancellor of the Exchequer

Foreword from The Plan for Growth. Published by HM Treasury and Department for Business, Innovation and Skills in March 2011 (P2)

The coalition Government handpicked eleven of the new Enterprise Zones.

- Black Country - I54 and Darlaston
- Derby, Derbyshire, Nottingham and Nottinghamshire - Nottingham (Boots Campus)
- Greater Birmingham and Solihull - Birmingham (Birmingham City Centre)
- Greater Manchester - Manchester (Airport)
- Leeds City Region - Leeds (Lower Aire Valley)
- Liverpool City Region - Liverpool (Mersey Waters)
- London - London (Royal Docks)
- North Eastern - River Tyne and Nissan site
- Sheffield City Region - Sheffield (The Modern Manufacturing and Technology Growth Area)
- Tees Valley - Tees Valley Enterprise Zone
- West of England - Bristol (Temple Quarter)

The remaining 10 golden tickets would be awarded after a competition, open to any region. Newly formed "Local Enterprise Partnerships" (LEP) were exclusively invited to submit bids for vacant and highly sought after Enterprise Zones.

The prospectus was uncompromising. Enterprise Zone status would only be given to "major cities and areas of significant untapped potential in places that have been dependent on the public sector."

"We want to ensure that Enterprise Zones will generally be based on `clean` sites with little or no business occupants. Targeting such sites will reduce the risks of simply favouring incumbent businesses with little added value to the economy of the area."

Enterprise Zone Prospectus

Department for Communities and Local Government – March 2011

The winning bids were announced on 17th August, 2011. The Coalition added that, rather than 10 golden tickets, "the strength of the applications from Local Enterprise Partnerships was such that Government has agreed to increase this invitation to 11."[100] The final Enterprise Zones were located in:

- Humber Estuary Renewable Energy Super Cluster

- Warrington - Daresbury Science Campus

- Cornwall - Newquay Aero Hub

- Gosport - The Solent Enterprise Zone at Daedalus Airfield

- Leicestershire - MIRA Technology Park in Hinckley

- Hereford - Rotherwas Enterprise Zone

- Discovery Park in Sandwich, Kent and Enterprise West Essex in Harlow

- Oxfordshire - Science Vale UK

- Northampton Waterside

- Cambridgeshire - Alconbury Airfield near Huntingdon

- Great Yarmouth in Norfolk, and Lowestoft in Suffolk.

This direct but select government intervention offered resident businesses a "rate discount worth up to £275,000 per business over a five year period." The Government would also "radically" simplify planning approval in these zones and guarantee super fast broadband.

A windfall for small and medium sized businesses? Department for Business Innovation and Skills statistics indicate over 90 percent of businesses had an average turnover less than £110,000 in 2009 – a figure less than half the rate discount available to each company. It does not take a mathematician to conclude Enterprise Zones were pitched at the richer organisations with more clout and employability. Albeit, association benefits would no doubt accrue for small businesses located in the vicinity and supply chain.

From April 2012, Local Authorities would be permitted to discount rates up to 100 percent for any organisation resident in an Enterprise Zone by April 2015. The Councils would not lose out, the Government agreed to replenish any discounts from central budgets and committed that future rate income from the Enterprise Zones could be retained locally for the next quarter of a century.

Private Council – LEP

"We will support the creation of Local Enterprise Partnerships - joint local authority-business bodies brought forward by local authorities themselves to promote local economic development - to replace Regional Development Agencies (RDAs)."

The Coalition: Our Programme for Government
Published by the Cabinet Office – May 2010

On 12th July, 2010, Mark Prisk MP, Minister for Small Business, announced, the "coalition Government are committed to replacing regional development agencies (RDAs) with Local Enterprise Partnerships (LEP)." Regional Development Agencies would be formally abolished in March 2012. But who or what was a LEP and how was it going to help small and medium sized businesses?

The coalition Government wanted to create "locally owned partnerships" to take the leading role in deciding economic "priorities" for their regions. These organisations would work to drive "economic growth and the creation of local jobs." The key differences between old Regional Development Agencies and the new Local Enterprise Partnerships were geography and demography, not purpose. These new bodies would be based on "more meaningful economic areas" rather than just the nine broad areas previously served by Regional Development Agencies. By the 13th May, 2011, Mark Prisk MP could already claim "33 partnerships in place covering 92 percent of all businesses in England."

Another key difference was leadership and the structure of the LEP Boards. Out went appointed public funded oligarchs to be replaced by

230

a mix of private sector entrepreneurs and councillors from Local Authorities. The make up and size of each individual Board was at the discretion of each area. Not surprisingly, a brief survey demonstrated that LEP Boards varied widely in both size and make up. Members include a representative from each local authority in the region, with the remaining members appointed from the private sector or academic institutions. Representation from the Chamber of Commerce and Federation of Small Businesses also featured. Public funded business support was pretty much non-existent.

Predictably, the final key difference for the Government was cost saving. The £2.2 billion annual budget for Regional Development Agencies would be cancelled by this partial privatisation of regional economic strategy.[101]

If you were a small business, the relationship already felt familiar. Small fish still don't make a big splash.

Regional Growth Fund

"This is a step change in the way regional growth is driven. And part of that step change is the Regional Growth Fund. We are saying to people – if you've got an idea to bring investment and wealth to your area, the £1.4 billion Regional Growth Fund is there to help make those good ideas happen."

Prime Minister David Cameron MP

Department for Business Innovation and Skills Press Release

28th October, 2010

In a remarkable circle of events, Prime Minister David Cameron appointed Lord Heseltine CH, founder of Business Link, to Chair the new Independent Advisory Panel assessing project proposals for the fund. Lord Heseltine was clear that the primary "object of the exercise is to stimulate people to create jobs in the private sector."[102] Each bidder had to demonstrate how their project would "stimulate enterprise" and "create additional sustainable private sector employment." The strength of each proposal was further enhanced if the project targeted areas "currently dependent on the public sector."

"We will accept bids from private bodies and public private partnerships across England. No sector is excluded from bidding. Each bid is in competition with the next. Even if you have a good bid it might not succeed if others are better."

Regional Growth Fund – Policies

Department for Business Innovation and Skills – 12th April, 2011

The new Local Enterprise Partnerships were actively "encouraged" by the Government to bid themselves for a share of this money, albeit "evidence of private sector investment" was a prerequisite. At the very least, the LEP were expected to "coordinate" any bids emanating from within their respective areas.

The Government set the minimum bid at £1 million, a relatively low sum in contrast to past schemes, designed to "encourage innovation" from smaller organisations. The first round of bidding took place on 21st January, 2011. 464 applications were received, applying for funding of £2.78 billion. Of these bids, 68% were for projects requiring less than £5 million funding, proving the decision to set a low entry point was working.

"I have always believed in the need to give real support to small businesses for whom bidding for £1m is way beyond what they could normally expect. That's why we are providing more than £150m to give targeted support to small businesses, which are the lifeblood of our economy."

The Rt Hon the Lord Heseltine CH

More than £450m investment for regional jobs and growth

Department for Business, Innovation and Skills – 12th April, 2011

In total, fifty proposals were accepted to the value of £450 million. Winners in the first round included General Motors Ltd, Durham County Cricket Club Holdings Ltd, Nissan Motor Manufacturing (UK) Limited, Proctor & Gamble Technical Centres Limited, Bentley Motors and Birmingham Chamber of Commerce on behalf of Birmingham City Council.[103]

The return on investment promised for this £450 million injection of public finance was 27,549 direct jobs and 96,654 indirect jobs in associated supply chains and local economies.[104] Indirect employment is always difficult to evidence. However, these figures suggest the cost to create each job was £3,623 of funding.

Region	Direct Jobs	Indirect Jobs
East Midlands South East Midlands	1730	3140
North East	5216	8367
North West	5533	2279
South East & East of England	427	361
South West	787	535
West Midlands	6193	34669
Yorkshire & Humber	7628	2716
Other bids – national	35	44587
TOTAL	27549	96654

Source: Regional Growth Fund Round 1 – Analysis.

Department for Business Innovation and Skills Website 8th August, 2011

The second round opened on 12th April, 2011, with the intention of allocating the remaining "bulk of the £1.4 billion" fund. This round of bidding ended on 1st July, 2011. 492 applications were received (requesting £3.3 billion). Once again, 71% of bids were less than £5 million in value, suggesting smaller businesses were engaged.

Successful bids were varied in nature and as promised, all projects were evaluated on their own merits. Examples of winning bids:

- Haribo factory expansion of existing site near Wakefield
- Vivaro van to be built at General Motors plant (Luton) safe guarding 1,500 jobs, helped by conditional RGF allocation
- Construction of manufacturing plant on Lotte Chemical site
- Construction of a link road to facilitate wider housing, industrial and commercial development south of Doncaster

"Round one is already helping local economies across the country and has attracted £2.5 billion of private sector investment. This will directly create or protect over 27,000 jobs, and secure around a further 100,000 jobs on related supply chains and in local economies. We welcome the bids received for the second round, and hope we can do even more this time."

Nick Clegg MP, Deputy Prime Minister

Second round of bids for Regional Growth Fund being considered

Department for Business, Innovation and Skills – 29th July, 2011

For perspective, the £1.4 billion Regional Growth Fund was equivalent to fully funding Business Link operations for a decade, helping at least five million small and medium sized businesses.

Bigger Better Business

"The Business Link regional advisory service will continue to offer advice and support to businesses until November 2011. After this time the regional advisory service will be abolished along with the Regional Development Agencies (RDAs). The Business Link website and the national helpline will continue to operate. Local Enterprise Partnerships (LEPs) will be expected to drive regional economic growth in the absence of the Business Link regional advisory service."

Business Link.gov.uk website - August 2011

The coalition Government published their vision for "Bigger Better Business" in January 2011. This document set out their economic strategy and tactics to be employed in support of small and medium sized businesses.

DIY Diagnosis

Even though the lights were going out for the advisory service in Business Links, the BusinessLink.gov.uk website was given utmost importance in the new blueprint for better business.

Far from being cut, the coalition Government committed to expanding this online content and improving functionality. Small businesses would have the option to tailor content to their needs. A larger selection of online diagnostic tools would be uploaded allowing entrepreneurs to submit their data online and receive automated diagnosis of their issues. In Business Links, prior to November 2011, these diagnostic reports typically highlighted a large number of issues and used links to further information to help find solutions. However, it was common for people using online diagnostics to call Business Link for face to face explanation.

Online information was scalable and relatively low cost. Public funded telephone and face to face business advice was no longer an attractive proposition, either ideologically or financially.

'Do it yourself' was the imposed new mantra for small businesses. However, just in case you were a DIY disaster, or one of the 24 percent of small and medium sized businesses the Government claimed were still offline, a new National Contact Centre was launched in November 2011.[105] Call centre staff would be available to direct you to the correct areas of the website, but would not be tasked or trained to provide tailored business advice. A small team of office bound advisers would be tasked to make up to 10,000 outbound calls per annum. This contract was worth over £9 million to the winning contractor Careline Services (in partnership with Business Enterprise Group), paid over a three year period.

"The helpline will play a vital role in supporting small businesses and start ups, especially those businesses that need help to access information available on the web."

Mark Prisk MP, Minister for Small Business

Department for Business Innovation and Enterprise Press Release - August 2011

Over half a million calls were expected from stuck customers.

Still Solutions

"Government's goal is to promote a strong, mixed economy which encourages high growth business to flourish. We are taking coordinated action to re-balance the economy and prodiving targeted assistance for manufacturing, emerging sectors, inward investment and international trade. The Solutions for Business Portfolio provides a range of publically funded products and services to help businesses. Overcome key changes."

Mark Prisk MP, Minister for Small Business

Department for Business Innovation and Enterprise Press Release - August 2011

The coalition Government retained the Solutions for Business portfolio of products created by the previous administration. However, a number of these products were revised and repackaged. For example, the Manufacturing Advisory Service was contracted to a new provider, as was the High Growth Coaching service. Manufacturing and engineering were still deemed critical to future economic recovery.

Fundementally, the thirteen original business support products remained untouched, available to any business that met the eligibility criteria designed to filter out all but the "high growth businesses."

With little else on offer, logic says all businesses need apply.

Mentors plus Me

The Bigger Better Business vision promised to replace public funded advisory services with an army of private sector mentors. The Government pledged to set up "a network of at least 40,000 experienced business mentors offering practical advice."

"We will work with the organisations that businesses respect and trust to ensure that information on how to run a business is provided by those who know and in most cases, those who have done it all before... We are working with the British Bankers Association, UK trade bodies and mentoring organisations to develop a single web-based gateway for mentoring so that potential mentors and mentees can find the right match for their needs."

Bigger Better Business, Helping Small Firms Start, Grow and Prosper
Department of Business Innovation and Skills – January 2011

In July 2011, the new mentoring website was launched on the domain Mentorsme.co.uk. This online network was "set up by the UK's five largest high street banks" - Barclays, HSBC, Lloyds Banking Group, Royal Bank of Scotland and Santander. These organisations pledged 10,000 mentors of their own to the scheme later on.

The creation of this website shunted the burden of responsibility for small business advice firmly back onto the private sector, saving an estimated £150 million per annum in Business Link funding. Over 13,500 unique visitors accessed the website in the first month online. When launched, the site offered access to 12,000 mentors, "offering both free and paid for mentoring", delivered by around 50 mentoring organisations.[106]

The take up of mentors, paid or otherwise, in the small business population remains to be seen. Businesses used to freebies would now have to accept personal advice with a price.

Coaching for Growth

For a lucky few businesses, access to face to face personal business advisers would not come to an end. Business Coaching for Growth was a new £173 million contract funded by the Government.

This support would commence January 2012 and cover a three years period.[107] The winning bidder would deliver a national free coaching service, but only for 10,000 business per annum, those entrepreneurs with the highest potential. The scheme would be delivered by "specialist private sector providers." The product offer included access to a personal coach to help businesses "address barriers to growth and to grow more rapidly." In the pilot programme, this typically involved up to ten days coaching per annum free of charge. The coach would focus on "investor readiness" and help to "commercially exploit Intellectal Property and Innovation." The coach would also help you network with investors, UK Trade and Investment (UKTI) and other business support groups. Customers in the programme would have access to a peer to peer network and facilities such as Technology Innovation Centres. A one person Business Link if you will, for better businesses only.

If you were an established small businesses, you had to evidence an ability and desire to "increase employment or turnover by 20 percent or more each year for three years." Start ups had to prove they could become "gazelles", able to achieve £1 million sales within three years or have 10 employees.[108]

If not, it was off to the Business Link website for some DIY diagnosis and some self-service.

EPILOGUE

PERSONAL BUSINESS

"The most serious barriers to success are those of a personal nature, not business. I have worked with husband and wife teams whose marriages broke due to the stress of running a small business. I have worked with family businesses where the rules of business are torn up and the potential for emotional conflict constantly simmers just below the surface. I have worked with entrepreneurs who have died in the middle of projects. I have even received a suicide note. These are the threats that end organisations and ruin lives. Life changing events brought on by the pressure of business."

Elliot Forte
Personal Business Adviser
Business Link - 1996 to 2011

Full Circle

Differences of opinion will always exist on how and whether government intervenes in the affairs of small businesses. These arguments are driven by a conflict of ideology as much as any economic justification. The resulting cycle of change creates an instability in industrial policy and more importantly, restricts the help available to small businesses. It is also a waste of tax payer funds as different initiatives launch, die and relaunch once memory fades. I hope this book can make a contribution to breaking this cycle, by illustrating how policy evolves and the impact any resulting interventions have on small businesses.

In 2011, the Conservative Liberal Democrat coalition implemented a business support strategy even less interventionist than the Thatcher era. It is true that the pressure of budget constraints forced their hand to some extent. These changes will impact on hundreds of thousands of small businesses. Even with a mixed reputation, over 750,000 small and medium sized businesses were engaging Business Link each year.[109] In my experience, without exception, every small business owner expressed surprise, then incredulity (followed by resignation) regarding the decision to scale down government funded advice, at a time when small businesses were most in need.

It remains to be seen whether handing the baton back to private sector consultancy and a "self-serving" Business Link website can deliver the hoped for improvements in quality of advice. I hope it will.

Small and medium sized enterprises account for over 99 percent of all businesses, over 55 percent of private sector employment and over 45 percent of private sector turnover.[110] Strategically, the success of all small and medium sized businesses is critical to an economic recovery and is in *everyone*'s interest. Nevermind any social responsibility there may be to support entrepreneurs (tax payers and voters) of all persuasions.

Ultimately, it is almost inevitable that the pendulum will swing back to a more interventionist policy which helps the wider business community, rather than just "gazelles", albeit is unlikely to do so until 2020.

Life Support

In a free market economy, public funded business support exists to stimulate the economic performance of the country. Economically, if there was no market failure there would be no case for intervention.

Yet, whilst politics and economics dominate the rhetoric, public funded business support is also about supporting an individual's hopes and aspirations, the acorn entrepreneurs that all have the potential to do better business. A business may become successful, profits may rise, people will be employed and lifestyles will improve. Conversely, some businesses fail, losses are made, debts are incurred and people lose their jobs. Families will suffer. Family circumstances, personal finance and the mental state of the individual leading the business, these complex and volatile issues are the real barriers to better business. Public funded advice addresses a market failure eternal in business, those most in need of a "business friend" are least able to pay.

Feedback from the customers of Business Link repeatedly cited the chance to speak openly to an independent person as the added value. This was a rare opportunity to share their issues and release the pent up isolation that afflicts every entrepreneur. A chance to speak with someone with nothing to sell but honest opinion and a listening ear, willing and able to say what needs to be said, even when that may be difficult to swallow. A value without measure and an element of the service that, seemingly, has so easily been overlooked.

I have encountered many challenges to growth whilst working closely with over one thousand small and medium sized businesses. However, the most serious barriers to success have always been those of a personal nature, not business. I have worked with husband and wife teams whose marriages broke due to the stress of running a small business. I have worked with family businesses where the rules of business are torn up and the potential for emotional conflict constantly simmers just below the surface. I have worked with entrepreneurs who have died in the middle of projects. I have even received a suicide note. These are the threats that end organisations and ruin lives.

Life changing events brought on by the pressure of business.

In the nineties, the Business Link for Norfolk agricultural team used to hand out a self-produced "yellow card" to entrepreneurs. This pocket-sized card listed three telephone numbers. For business support call Business Link. For Agricultural advice call the National Farmers Union. The third number was the telephone number for the Samaritans. I was told this simple card had saved lives. I have never forgotten my emotions when I first saw the "yellow card." Is there any better illustration of the heavy responsibility that rests on all advisers, particularly those helping the owners of small businesses?

In 1992, Lord Heseltine first conceived the need for small businesses to have a "trusted friend." Who will perform this role in a private sector landscape of business support? Paid consultants, hungry competitors, online forums?

Steady State of Mind

Emotions affect business performance.

It is the violently shifting state of a business mind that is the greatest determinant of entrepreneurial performance, not being able to read a profit and loss sheet or understand marketing. These skills are important but count for nothing in the absence of enterprise.

Exposing small business owners to entrepreneurial thinking is most effective when you know a person's individual aspirations, their personal circumances (however sensitive) and you can create an atmosphere of trust. Money muddies these waters. Yet this, in my view, is the most valuable output from an impartial government funded advisory service.

Just marginally changing the way people think about themselves and their business potential is high impact and long term. I have met £1,000,000 entrepreneurs, who consider themselves business failures and others who have tens of thousands of pounds on credit cards but consider themselves a success. These states of mind are both dangerous as they unconciously fuel a denial of their own entrepreneurial capacity. One has money but remains unfulfilled and unaware of their potential for business growth (creating jobs). The other is over stretched and heading for a fall (costing jobs). Knowing yourself is virtually impossible when you look out and use only one set of eyes.

A public funded business advisory service delivered clear water, no money changed hands between the small business and adviser. It was a relationship based purely on helping the small business. This created an environment where advisers could challenge entrepreneurs without fear. That's not to say all the advisers had the capability, inclination or motivation to do so. But many did.

I consider myself extremely fortunate to have had the opportunity to work with over a thousand businesses in this open atmosphere. From these experiences and observations, I developed a strong belief in the existance of a *steady state* of mind, an entrepreneurial sweet spot. In chemistry, a steady state is where all variables are constant, in spite of ongoing processes that strive to change them. For the entrepreneur these processes eminate from every day life. The challenge is to help individuals recognise when these changes have created an unconcious shift away from this optimal state of mind. I believe addressing this issue is how you create a long term legacy for better business.

Holding up this mirror to small business entrepreneurs is a very risky process, and if not carefully managed, can open up a can of worms that eats away at the business long after the intervention is complete. Yet this issue is the main barrier to performance at the core of every business. When these complex issues are ignored, either through fear or lack of resource, this is wrong, morally and economically.

Nevermind the economy, when it comes to peoples' lives a short sharp intervention is plainly irresponsible.

At the risk of ending on a negative, the gradual dehumanisation of small and medium sized business is the most concerning legacy of a generation of government sponsored business support. The idea that an entrepreneur needs a trusted "friend" is an old joke, an outdated philosophy for another era. In today's world of business dragons and ambitious apprentices, this belief has given way to a more selective intervention by a new Government targeting "gazelles", winners not losers. A survival of the fittest philosophy that is by it's very nature – cold hearted.

Schools Out

The coalition Government has implemented the majority of recommendations in the Richard Report. However, the recommended shake up of education and enterprise in schools is conspicuously absent in their Plan for Growth.

Until entrepreneurs of the future are properly prepared for a life of enterprise, the need for intervention will never subside. Every young person will step on the learning curve at the lowest point and experience the shell shock of first time business. An experience that some will survive and grow, others will survive but flounder and a few will not survive at all.

Intervention in business is not the solution. This approach tackles the symptoms, not the source, of entrepreneurial weakness. Reduce dependency early by reducing a need for corrective business support.

Traditional teaching of business studies, economics, management degrees, MBA doesn't prepare a person for the positive and negative emotions that attack the senses in enterprise, barriers to maintaining an entrepreneurial mind.

In my view, the main conclusion from the Intervention story must be Doug Richard's own - help future entrepreneurs help themselves.

The Battle for Better Business

Business Link had many faults, regardless of whether you think this degree of intervention was acceptable ideologically. In a human system there will always be problems. However, anyone who cares about small business must acknowledge the sheer scale of engagement that took place and the learning that this *people to people* contact must have generated. This knowledge was scattered to the wind on November 25th, 2011, when the Government finally closed the Business Link advisory service, quietly erasing 18 years of intervention from history.

Intervention, the Battle for Better Business is a humble attempt to chronicle these events, to do justice to the millions of small businesses that were Business Link customers and the thousands of business advisers (public and private funded) who worked to build better business.

Intervene boldly in education.

Make a better life in business.

....

Further reading and discussion:

www.battleforbetterbusiness.co.uk

APPENDIX

HESELTINE

2011

"My Party would not take kindly to the arguments that you should have these in depth support systems. In truth, when I did it, I did comprehensive presentations to Conservative back benchers so that they could see what I believed an industrial policy was about. What they felt it was likely to be about were things like backing winners, or subsidising losers.

Now I certainly wasn't in favour of the latter."

The Rt Hon the Lord Heseltine CH
Chairman of the Independent Advisory Board for the Regional Growth Fund.
Interview with author at Haymarket Head Office - Hammersmith, London
8th June, 2011

In 1992, Lord Heseltine was President of the Board of Trade within John Major's Conservative Government and subsequently became Deputy Prime Minister.

Lord Heseltine was responsible for developing the vision for Business Link and is credited widely as founder of the network.

In 2011, Prime Minister David Cameron appointed Lord Heseltine as Chair of the Independent Advisory Panel coordinating the Regional Growth Fund, a £1.4 billion investment by the Government to create jobs in the private sector. As a significant element of the Coalition's Plan for Growth, a generation after the start of Business Link, and in the deepest economic crisis, Lord Heseltine was once again at the heart of the intervention agenda.

On 8th June, 2011, Lord Heseltine agreed to meet the author to discuss Business Link and the issue of government intervention.

The following text is a transcript taken from that interview.

 (111)    (112)

Rt Hon the Lord Heseltine CH   Elliot H. Forte

[LH]   [EF]

Manager vs. Entrepreneur

EF   I have worked with approximately three thousand small and medium sized businesses.

What strikes me that whole time is that Business Link policy was always about management improvement. In *every* single company that I met it wasn't about management first, it was about the leader's capability to be entrepreneurial. So I would go into a company and talk about management, but actually it was more about scope to be enterprising.

I just wondered why that was, or even if that was the case?

LH   I'm not sure I know how you distinguish between the two.

Open Minds

EF   I have been stimulating business improvement in terms of nuts and bolts, the mechanics of business.

What I think was actually happening when speaking to businesses is I was organically having a conversation with the entrepreneur about enterprise, about risk, about scenarios and trying to widen their scope.

I may have gone way beyond the remit (of Business Link). However, I know this is what most advisers would do, try to open up their scope of what entrepreneurs can do, which was never a specific Business Link service.

I believe that was where the true value was, certainly from customer feedback.

Is that what you anticipated? Was that beyond the remit?

LH   No, I think that it's within the remit, in the fact that there was a remit. The remit I've described was to be a friend in need, to do what you could to answer their questions.

What the form of the questions were and what opportunities of dialogue would unfold, that was never prescriptive. We never tried to tell anyone how to conduct an interview or what to look for.

EF   Do you think you should have been prescriptive about that particular aspect?

LH   No, I don't.

You were an experienced friend that they wanted to talk to.

Small and Medium

EF   The other thing that strikes me, quite starkly, is that I would read the policy discussions and they would describe small to medium sized businesses that looked *nothing* like the people I was seeing.

These reports were describing companies that have the sophistication to actually adopt business improvement practice quite rapidly, they would make assumptions on their knowledge of finance and they would make assumptions on their knowledge of management.

That was more or less across the board not what I found when talking to people. I understand small to medium sized business is a large banding.

I would go and meet these business people to talk about information diagnostic and brokerage, and the main findings were forget the nuts and bolts, the basics were not there to actually push it on as fast as people expected us to.

Is that something you would agree with, that the reality doesn't necessarily match the research, and if not why not?

LH   Well I couldn't know. I've never seen the research.

All I know is that I can remember being told that something like a hundred thousand enquiries were coming through to Business Link in a year. That indicated to me that there was a demand out there.

We didn't set out to serve a certain sector or a certain scale of business. We were there as a coordinated advisory business, that's what we thought the idea was, coordinating public information and giving advice about anything anyone wanted to raise, from someone who'd had some business experience. A lot the advice I would have imagined at the early stage would have gone to people employing 2 to 5 people.

Pathetic State

EF   In 1997, Patricia Hewitt said that Business Link was in a "pathetic state" when the Labour Party came to power. That's not how I recall the situation. But it is a quote from someone significant, someone who had your role in fact.

How do you remember it?

LH   Well, if you set up a business, an organisation like that, you are going to get a lot of criticism.

You are going to get criticisms *particularly* about the people who you are using to give advice, because people will say they don't have any real experience, they don't have any real knowledge, and those are the people that will create the image in too easy a way.

And if the Press want to start picking that up, then it gets in the public mind.

My information is that we got a lot of enquiries, there was a demand and I personally never saw any serious complaints. I *heard* about press criticism but I've long since learned to discount press criticism.

You have to aim off for that sort of selective reporting.

Chamber Resistance

EF   You started Business Link, which brought together different support agencies that are relatively fragmented, with an express remit to help businesses invest in knowledge and stimulate the market.

           Yet from start to finish, these agencies have repeatedly expressed the core criticism of lack of value.

           Why would they do that?

LH   Why would who do it?

EF   I'll give you some examples. The Chamber of Commerce was quite a voracious critic of Business Link, even though they were often part of it.

LH   Well I think they regarded Business Link as an intrusion into their fiefdom. But the reason we created Business Link was because the Chambers weren't doing a good enough job.

           So there was a tension there from the beginning.

EF   In which respect weren't they doing a good enough job?

LH   They themselves should have set up this combined advisory service. They should have gone to Government and said, look you've got all these services, work with us and create the one stop shop. That's what they should have done.

           We did it for them.

           But there was resistance in the earlier days and there were criticisms from the Chambers. That doesn't mean to say the Chambers were right.

Get Off Our Backs

EF Can I ask you about a couple more organisations?

LH Yes.

EF The Federation of Small Businesses?

LH Well they would be 'Get Off Our Backs' school of thinking. They would believe that small business doesn't need that sort of public advice.

I don't agree with that particular judgement. The scale of the enquiries reveals the demand was there.

We can argue about whether the quality of the service was good enough. But my view would have been that argument could only lead to a debate about how you could improve it, not closing it down.

EF One more agency, one I think you were integral to actually setting up. The Enterprise Agencies.

LH Well the Enterprise Agencies were not so much me; it was Geoffrey Howe. And… no, I'm so sorry, I am talking about Enterprise Zones. Enterprise Agencies, what were they?

EF You did the Community in the Business scheme in the 80s, and the Enterprise Agencies evolved from that.

LH I think we did have something to do with them. They were in the very early 80s weren't they? I think we seconded an official to help. Look, I better say it was a long time ago.

They certainly weren't a central part of what we were doing. But I think that we did help a bit.

EF   Out of a thousand companies that I have personally worked with, I would estimate one in thirty hold any strategy meetings at all, one in two hundred have a non-executive Director of any kind, while I am being terribly cynical, this is often an accountant who'd done them a favour or a friend. Not what I imagine the role to be.

One in a thousand would actually be running a Board, whether it is right or wrong, on Institute of Directors principles. So my conclusion is that in small business we have a nation of managers not Directors at Board level.

Why did Government not target this issue?

LH   Well. On that you would have two schools of thought.

You would have the left wing, who wouldn't have any real interest in effective management of the capitalist system... and you would have a very powerful element on the right wing of politics that would think it's a matter for the capitalist system to manage itself and government intervention, as they would call it, would be very unattractive, unlikely to achieve anything and bureaucratic.

So you have a very polarised approach to the sort of issues you're asking me about. I don't share that approach.

I think that in many of our competitor countries there are very powerful organisations helping small to medium sized businesses, very effectively. The whole issue of public law status on the continent is an example of that. But the climate here would be very hostile to it, including the climate of organisations that claim to represent small businesses.

EF   Why would that be? I mean it's the top of the tree isn't it. A significant percentage of people at the top lack an understanding to effectively govern or direct small businesses. So everything below must not be as good as it could be. Why would you resist addressing that?

LH   Well I didn't resist it. I set up.

EF   Yes, but why would everyone else?

LH   Because the business climate of either overbearing intervention which comes from the left, or non-intervention which comes from the right. That's two very polarised positions, which I don't share.

My Party would not take kindly to the arguments that you should have these in depth support systems.

In truth, when I did it, I did comprehensive presentations to Conservative back benchers so that they could see what I believed an industrial policy was about.

What they felt it was likely to be about were things like backing winners, or subsidising losers. Now I wasn't in favour of certainly the latter, but once I had done the presentations I had no complaints. But I'm deeply aware that there is a very substantial body of opinion, which would reflect itself in many of the representative organisations and in many of the newspapers, the populist newspapers I should say, which would be, very suspicious of anything that smacked of interventionism.

Or industrial strategy is another non-word, a non-idea. But I believe in industrial strategy.

Unanswerable Case

EF   In 2011, Dr. Vince Cable MP said "Business Link was widely criticised by the businesses for which it was designed. It was a very ineffective system of business support. Not a successful scheme and it was outdated for the 21st century."

Do you think Business Link was a successful scheme?
Why?

LH   I haven't any doubt that in the days when I was involved, and you've got to remember now we are going back to the early and mid 90s, it was successful and it was needed.

What I am hesitant to pass judgement about, is what is now necessary because I am fully aware that the web and electronic data transmission has taken a quantum leap since I was involved in this field. So a lot of information services could now be delivered through centralised one-stop web shops that we didn't understand in the 90s.

EF   And the concept is intervention, support the Small and Medium sized Enterprise market and contribute to the national economy. Is that right?

LH   I think that there's an unanswerable case for giving advisory support to small to medium sized companies, to help improve their performance, to answer questions, to be a sympathetic spectator if you like, in a way that most competitor economies provide in one way or another.

....

EF   Would you change anything about what happened?

LH   At the beginning?

EF   Yes, that set the scene for whatever happened afterwards.

LH   I am probably in favour of public law status. Which means that businesses (must) register with their Chamber, and the Chamber's therefore much richer, and can give far more impressive support, which they do on the continent. If you travel overseas you see the support the Chambers give to German or French industry. It is amazing, huge fairs and exhibitions and that sort of thing.

EF   Over the last twenty years, millions of pounds have been invested in people working at the coalface for Business Link. Millions of pounds of training that was an investment way beyond what a consultancy would fund.

In Business Link you've got people who have volume insight, people who have personally been inside a thousand boardrooms, on the inside of small business and as you said, the trusted friend. A relationship with businesses where they will tell you anything, and they do.

You've got a workforce right now of about two thousand advisers, albeit an expensive workforce.

On November 25th that knowledge asset, a tax-funded asset, will be scattered to the wind.

Why would some effort not be made to capture what's there because I don't see those people in the vision for the future?

LH   Well I can't answer that question. Because it sounds to me you just described Business Link with different names.

EF   I think that's an answer in itself isn't it.

LH   Yes. <Pause>

But that's what Governments do.

NOTES AND REFERENCES

(1)   Michael Heseltine. House of Commons Hansard Debates. 21st July, 1994

(2)   Wren, C and Storey, D J. Evaluating the effect of soft business support upon small firm performance. Oxford Economic Papers 54. 2002.

(3)   Bennett, R.J. and Robson P.J.A. Changing use of external business advice and Government support during the 1990s. Regional Studies 37. 2003.

(4)   Saal, D; Mole, K; Roper, S and Hart, M. Economic Impact Study of Business Link Local Service. Project Report. Department for Business Enterprise and Regulatory Reform. 2006.

(5)   Michael Heseltine, Life in the Jungle, Hodder & Stoughton, 2000

(6)   Oral Answers in House of Commons Sitting. Hansard. 5th April, 1995.

(7)   Competitiveness: Forging Ahead (Cm 2867). Great Britain. Dept. of Trade and Industry, Publisher HMSO, 1995

(8)   Robert Gray. UK Business Link Proves its Worth. Published in Management Today magazine. 1st October, 1997.

(9)   Report on Business Link. The Institute of Directors. 1996

(10) Robert Gray. UK Business Link Proves its Worth. Published in Management Today magazine. 1st October, 1997.

(11) Robert Gray. UK Business Link Proves its Worth. Published in Management Today magazine. 1st October, 1997.

(12) Robert Gray. UK Business Link Proves its Worth. Published in Management Today magazine. 1st October, 1997.

(13) Creating the Enterprise Centre of Europe. DTI Competitiveness White Paper. 1996

(14) House of Commons Hansard Written Answers. 11th October, 2010

(15) Robert Gray. UK Business Link Proves its Worth. Published in Management Today magazine. 1st October, 1997.

(16) Competitiveness: How the best UK companies are winning. Confederation of British Industry / Department of Trade and Industry. 1994.

(17) Our Competitive Future: Building the Knowledge Driven Economy (Cm. 4167) Great Britain. Dept. of Trade & Industry. December 1998.

(18) Our Competitive Future. Building the Knowledge Driven Economy: Drivers of demand in the digital economy. December 1998.

(19) http://www.britishchambers.org.uk/general/about-the-british-chambers-of-commerce.html. 17th October, 2011.

(20) http://www.fsb.org.uk/about. 17th October, 2011.

(21) British Chambers of Commerce. National Benchmarking Survey 2010. www.britishchambers.org.uk/toolkit/national_rankings_2010-pdf.html

(22) Mark Prisk MP, Minister of State for Business and Enterprise. Response to question from Chuka Umunna MP. http://www.theyworkforyou.com. Hansard source. Citation: HC Deb, 28th June, 2011, c718W.

(23) British Chambers of Commerce. The Future Chamber: Integrated Local Business Support for 2000 and Beyond. 1997.

(24) Robert Gray. UK Business Link Proves its Worth. Published in Management Today magazine. 1st October, 1997.

(25) Mr Lindsay Hoyle, House of Commons Select Committee - Trade and Industry. Minutes of Evidence. 2nd June, 1998

(26) House of Commons Select Committee - Trade and Industry. Minutes of Evidence. 2nd June, 1998

(27) Public and Corporate Economic Consultants (PACEC). Business Links - Value for Money Evaluation. October 1998

(28) Department of Trade and Industry. Enhanced Business Links - a Vision for the 21st Century. 8th October, 1997.

(29) Department of Trade and Industry. Enhanced Business Links - a Vision for the 21st Century. 8th October, 1997.

(30) Personal Business Adviser Survey (Business Link 2010)

(31) Department of Trade and Industry. Enhanced Business Links - a Vision for the 21st Century. 8 October, 1997.

(32) Department of Trade and Industry. Enhanced Business Links - a Vision for the 21st Century. 8 October, 1997.

(33) Public and Corporate Economic Consultants (PACEC). Business Links - Value for Money Evaluation. October 1998

(34) Justice Louis Dembitz Brandeis. Born November 13, 1856. Died October 5, 1941

(35) Ms Haf Merrifield, House of Commons Trade and Industry Commons Select Committee – Minutes of Evidence. 2nd May, 2001

(36) Certificate in Company Direction (2010) – www.iod.com. Studied by author at Exeter University.

(37) Robert Gray. UK Business Link Proves its Worth. Published in Management Today magazine. 1st October, 1997

(38) House of Commons Select Committee - Trade and Industry. Minutes of Evidence. 2nd June, 1998

(39) Evaluation of Business Links. A report prepared by Ernst and Young on behalf of the Department of Trade and Industry. 1996.

(40) "When there were 80 plus Business Links we were involved with between 35 and 40 of them. When it reduced to 45 Links we were involved with over 20 of them. When it reduced to 9 we were involved with 4 of them." - Information supplied by John McMahon of www.forum21.co.uk. 27th September, 2011

(41) Support Services for SMEs: does the "franchisee" make a difference to the Business Link offer? Bennett R, Robson P, 2004 Environment and Planning C 22 859-880

(42) Bennett, R.J. and Robson P. Business Link: Use, satisfaction and the influence of local governance regime, Policy Studies, 24, 163-186. 2003.

(43) Mole, K; Roper, S and Hart, M. Economic Impact Study of Business Link Local Service. Project Report. Department for Business Enterprise and Regulatory Reform. 2006.

(44) The Rt Hon the Lord Heseltine CH. Interview with author at Haymarket Head Office, Hammersmith – 8th June, 2011

(45) Nigel Griffiths MP, Minister for Small Business. House of Commons Hansard Written Answers. 20th January, 2004

(46) "Only around half of the respondents to the survey indicated that the full effect of assistance would be realised within 12 months." Saal, D; Mole, K; Roper, S and Hart, M. Economic Impact Study of Business Link Local Service. Project Report. Department for Business Enterprise and Regulatory Reform. 2006.

(47) Nigel Griffiths MP, Minister for Small Business. House of Commons Hansard Written Answers. 27 February, 2004

(48) House of Commons Trade and Industry Commons Select Committee – Minutes of Evidence. 2nd May, 2001

(49) Patricia Hewitt MP, Minutes of Evidence taken before the Trade and Industry Committee. 12th December, 2001

(50) Irwin Grayson Associates website (www.irwingrayson.com) 2011.

(51) House of Commons Hansard Written Answers. 21st July, 2004

(52) House of Commons Hansard Written Answers. 20th October, 2004.

(53) House of Commons Hansard Written Answers. 23rd July, 2002.

(54) House of Commons Hansard Written Answers. 16th November, 2004.

(55) Neely, A.; Szwejczewski, M.; Jarrar, Y. Closing the Gap 3. DTI Business Link and Cranfield University. 20th September, 2002.

(56) Nigel Griffiths MP. House of Commons Debate – Written Answers to Questions. 7th December, 2004.

(57) Department for Business Enterprise and Regulatory Reform (BERR) Annual Report and Accounts 2008 to 2009. July 2009

(58) House of Commons Written Answers. 11th October, 2010.

(59) House of Commons Debate. Written Answers to Questions. 19th September, 2002.

(60) House of Commons Debate. Written Answers to Questions. 19th September, 2002.

(61) www.archive.org (2011)

(62) House of Commons Debate. Written Answers to Questions. 19th September, 2002.

(63) www.archive.org (2011)

(64) House of Commons Hansard Written Answers. 5th July, 2007.

(65) Reporting on Progress: Central government websites 2009/10. Central Office of Information (COI). 2010

(66) http://www.businesslink.gov.uk - 18th October, 2011.

(67) Reporting on Progress: Central Government Websites 2009 – 2010. Central Office of Information. 2010.

(68) BusinessLink.gov.uk: Annual Review 2009-2010.

(69) www.archive.org (2011)

(70) House of Commons Trade and Industry Committee: Support to Businesses from Regional Development Agencies. Fifth Report of Session 2003–04. Printed 11th May, 2004

(71) Mr Martin Wyn Griffith, House of Commons Trade and Industry Minutes of Evidence. 6th January, 2004

(72) House of Commons Business and Enterprise. Minutes of Evidence. Session 2007-08. 20th November, 2007.

(73) Learning and Skills Council Grant Letter for 2009-2010.

(74) House of Commons Hansard Written Answers. 12th October, 2009.

(75) Press Release: Help for employers to prepare for the upturn. Department for Business Enterprise and Regulatory Reform BERR. 1st April, 2009.

(76) House of Commons Written Answers. 27th April, 2009.

(77) Cowling M, Oakley J. Globally Competitive Business Environment Report 09/1357, Department for Business, Innovation and Skills. Early Assessment of the Impact of Business Link Health Checks. Nov. 2009.

(78) House of Commons Hansard Written Answers. 12th October, 2009

(79) The Forum 21 Model - Further information at www.forum21.co.uk

(80) House of Commons Hansard Written Answers. 27th January, 2010.

(81) House of Commons Hansard Written Answers. 12th October, 2009.

(82) House of Commons Hansard Written Answers. 12th October, 2009.

(83) Business Payment Support Service: An Official Statistics Release. HM Revenue and Customers (Knowledge, Analysis and Intelligence Directorate). July 2011

(84) http://www.swloansfund.co.uk/ - 18th October, 2011

(85) House of Commons Hansard Written Answers. 1st February, 2010

(86) Damian Waters, Regional Director, Confederation of British Industry North West. House of Commons North West Regional Committee - Minutes of Evidence. The impact of the current economic situation on the North West and the Government's response. Session 2008-09. Oral evidence taken 15th June, 2009.

(87) House of Commons Hansard Debates. 10th March, 2009.

(88) Lord Mandelson announces Government guaranteeing more than £1m loans a day. Department for Business, Enterprise and Regulatory Reform: News Release issued by Central Office of Information (COI) News Distribution Service. 20th February, 2009.

(89) Small Business and Government: The Richard Report. Submission to Shadow Cabinet (Conservative) by Doug Richard. 8th May, 2008

(90) Mark Prisk MP, Minister of State for Business and Enterprise. Response to question from Chuka Umunna MP. 28th June, 2011 http://www.theyworkforyou.com. Hansard source (Citation: HC Deb, 28th June, 2011, c718W).

(91) Mark Prisk MP, Minister of State for Business and Enterprise. Response to question from Chuka Umunna MP. 28th June, 2011 http://www.theyworkforyou.com. Hansard source (Citation: HC Deb, 28th June, 2011, c719W).

(92) The Rt Hon the Lord Heseltine CH. Interview with author at Haymarket Head Office, Hammersmith. 8th June, 2011.

(93) Mark Prisk MP, Minister of State for Business and Enterprise. Response to question from Chuka Umunna MP. 28th June, 2011 http://www.theyworkforyou.com. Hansard source (Citation: HC Deb, 28th June, 2011, c718W).

(94) Lords Hansard text. 24th March, 2011.

(95) Statement by Mark Prisk MP, Secretary of State for Business, Innovation and Skills. House of Commons Debate Written Answers. 6th July, 2010.

(96) Mark Prisk MP, Minister of State for Business and Enterprise. Response to question from Chuka Umunna MP. 28th June, 2011 http://www.theyworkforyou.com. Hansard source (Citation: HC Deb, 28th June, 2011, c718W).

(97) HM Treasury and Department for Business Innovation and Skills. The Plan for Growth. March 2011.

(98) HM Treasury and Department for Business Innovation and Skills. The Plan for Growth. March 2011.

(99) George Osborne MP: We're building a better future for Britain. The Chancellor's speech to Conservative Party Spring Forum in Cardiff. 5th March, 2011.

(100) Press notice issued by the Communities and Local Government website – http://www.communities.gov.uk - 17th August, 2011.

(101) Finance and governance of Regional Development Agencies. http://www.bis.gov.uk/policies/economic-development/englands-regional-development-agencies/rda-finance-and-governance.

(102) Lord Heseltine to oversee Regional Growth Fund. Conservative Party Website (news section). 28th October, 2010.

(103) Regional Growth Fund Round 1 – Analysis. Department for Business Innovation and Skills Website. 8th August, 2011.

(104) Regional Growth Fund Round 1 – Analysis. Department for Business Innovation and Skills Website. 8th August, 2011.

(105) Bigger, Better Business. Helping Small Firms Start, Grow and Prosper. Department for Business, Innovation and Skills. January 2011. Annual Small Business Survey, 2007/08, BIS 2009.

(106) National Initiative Briefing: Launch of mentorsme.co.uk. Department of Business, Innovation and Skills. 4th July, 2011.

(107) PublicTenders.net. Tender: UK-London: business and management consultancy and related services. 8th April, 2011.

(108) http://www.bis.gov.uk. Coaching for High Growth SMEs. 2011.

(109) Mark Prisk MP, Minister of State for Business and Enterprise. Response to question from Chuka Umunna MP. 28th June, 2011 http://www.theyworkforyou.com. Hansard source (Citation: HC Deb, 28th June, 2011, c718W).

(110) Department for Business Innovation and Skills. Statistical Press Release. http://stats.bis.gov.uk. 13th October, 2010.

(111) Photo Credit: www.haymarket.com. 12th October, 2011.

(112) Photo Credit: www.mattjessop.com / www.china-fleet.co.uk. 13th October, 2011.

www.ingramcontent.com/pod-product-compliance
Lightning Source LLC
Chambersburg PA
CBHW031831170526
45157CB00001B/265